Lessons Beneath the Mask

From Pain to Promise

By Reuel Barksdale

D1264150

Copyright©2017 by The Gold Standard Initiative
6956 East Broad Street
Suite 202
Columbus, Ohio 43213

Contributors:
"Dreams Do Come True" by Roya Masaebi
"I Started From the Bottom" by James Witherspoon
"Monsters in the Pews" by Jill Lundy
"Define Yourself" by Reuel Barksdale

Editor and publishing consultant: Joylynn M. Ross
Co-editor: Reuel Barksdale

Cover Design: David Pacheco
Photographer: Anthony Hairston
Booking Manager: Kesha Brown (tgsinitiative@gmail.com)

Library of Congress Cataloging-in-Publication: 2017936262

ISBN: 978-0-9987970-0-7

First Printing April 2017

10 9 8 7 6 5 4 3 2 1

Manufactured in the United States of America

Dedication

This book is dedicated to everyone who ever felt like giving up. If you are reading this page, this book was written for you.

TABLE OF CONTENTS

TABLE OF CONTENTS (Continued)

Foreword

There is a power and presence in you that can overcome anything that you are facing now, or in the future. *Lessons beneath the Mask* allows us to take a journey with four individuals whose life examples prove "Greater is he that is in you than he that is in the world."

Many statistics tell us each year we go through, that we or someone we care about will experience at least three tragedies. L.C. Robinson once said, "Things may happen around you and things may happen to you, but the only thing that really counts is what happens in you."

The following four stories illustrate we are more powerful than we know. These individuals convinced me even though I've been fighting cancer for over 21 years, I haven't gone through anything. This book will change your life as it has mine. Each chapter will remind you to live each day from a place of gratitude and faith. These are stories of courage, determination, and what it means to be unstoppable. All I could say after I read this book as I slid out of my bed to my knees with tears in my eyes was, "To God be the Glory."

-Les Brown

Introduction

Life requires that we consider a series of questions. What is the essence of life? Why are we here? What is truth and what truths should inform our lives? Are we the end result of some arbitrary cosmic explosion, or is there a master plan that guides our journey? Are we responsible for what happens to us, or are we simply pawns in the greater scheme of things? The contemplation of these and many other basic questions are at the center of life's experiences

Without an understanding of what is true, our lives are degraded into a series of meaningless occurrences. We seek to answer these questions in multiple situations and experiences.

The answers of meaning are declared, debated, and supposedly determined in our institutions of religion, politics, the sciences, and the arts. Our personal lives, even in childhood, wrestle with life's questions.

"She loves me. She loves me not."

As children, we believe that whatever our parents and authority figures declare to be true is, in fact, absolute truth. As youth, we rarely question the declarations of religious, political, or educational leaders. Our truths are provided for our unquestioned acceptance. There is little opportunity or expectation in our religious, political, or educational institutions for children to question what is presented as truth. The meanings and realities of life are then often defined by the framers of our childhood.

Life, however, soon teaches the child that there is no Santa Claus or Tooth Fairy. We may begin to develop political and religious opinions that differ from the deeply held beliefs of our parents and community leaders. We become aware of the failings and flaws of leadership figures who were, in our recent lives, seen as infallible. The shortcomings of our political, religious, and community leaders are displayed across the headlines and social media outlets. Once the invincibility of our leaders is exposed, it is a short journey to the questioning of the truths of which they declared to be absolute. In our adolescent years, we may develop friendships or acquaintances of which our parents do not approve. The adolescent child in school is exposed to different cultures, races, religions, political beliefs, and ways of life. These diversities are often the genesis of the child's exploration into their determination of what will be their own definitions of life and its fundamental truths.

A great truth that I have discovered is that no matter what one is going through, there is someone at some time who experienced a similar situation, and that someone at some point in time triumphed through the situation that seemed so hopeless. Many times we feel that the task in front of us is greater than the talent within us because we consider our situation to be uniquely unbearable. But what if the tormented individual could go to a source that would show life situations similar to their own where individuals were able to make it and indeed triumph? What if there were modern day examples of real people in really horrible situations that had somehow triumphed?

What if the hopeless, helpless situation was given hope and help? What if there was a way out?

As I was preparing the completion of this book, I shared with a friend of mine the premise of this work as being an opportunity to share a series of success stories with the reader. I wanted to write an inspirational book that would encourage the reader to persevere through life's most difficult challenges. My thought was that if I could show you, the reader, someone who had labored through a situation similar to your own and won, then you would, through their experience, be encouraged that you too could win.

I have always believed that each of us is born with a purpose that sometimes fades because of the harsh challenges of life. It seemed to me that life was full of sometimes painful processes that made the promise and purpose of life fade. I have seen too many people (because of the pain of life) reduced to questioning the very meaning of life. My friend shared a scripture with me that significantly changed the premise of what I am now sharing with you.

There is a particular Bible scripture that has clarified my purpose for writing this book:

"For I know the plans I have for you, declares the LORD, plans to prosper you and not to harm you, plans to give you hope and a future" Jeremiah 29:11 (NIV).

There are several interesting things about this scripture:

1. The scripture declares there is a God who cares enough about the affairs of men to actually plan their future. This means there must be a divine purpose for life, and that purpose is designed by God Himself. If God Himself has created a plan for my life, I can rest assured in the fact that I am not powerful enough to screw up God's plans for my life.

2. The scripture is written to and about a people that, because of their rebellion against God, are in a situation of dark despair. Their spiritual leaders have falsely prophesied, and their captors have viciously destroyed their political leaders. They would eventually spend 70 years in captivity. Yet, in this hopeless condition, they are given the promise of a plan.

3. There is a guarantee that God has no desire to cause harm to his people, and that despite the pain of their process, the promise of their future was one of prosperity and hope.

These truths have allowed me to refocus this book. The focus is not on the pain of the people, but on the promise of a plan. The good news is that no matter the pain of our current situation, we may rest in the existence of a plan.

I purposely did not qualify this truth to be exclusive to the Christian, believer, or the person in good standing with their religious organization. A quick review of the scriptures allows me to conclude that there was a plan for Saul before he became Paul. There was a plan

5

for each of the apostles before they accepted the call to follow. There was a plan for the woman at the well before she ran with the evangelistic call to "come see a man." I may not know you personally, but my guess is there have been times when you wondered about your future. You may have felt your current situation was so hopeless that throwing in the towel was your only viable option.

I offer the following stories in a search for truth, the truth about a plan that will give you a reason to hope. I do not suggest this work to be all inclusive. My hope, however, is that as you read through these pages, the truth learned through the experiences of others will assist you in the identification of your own absolute truth. The stories you will read are stories of real people who have encountered real life experiences. In the process, they discovered there was always a sometimes hidden, but very real plan. They each now appreciate this truth.

-Reuel Barksdale

Part I

"Dreams Do Come True"

(Roya Masaebi's Story)

Chapter One
Childhood Nightmares

A child of six years should not see certain things. I remember my mother grabbing my hand as we ran from my dad's demolished store. The ground was shaking and there was a horrible deafening roar whose origins my ears could not define. As we ran up the road of our village in a desperate attempt to find our way home, I saw bodies on the side of the road. A little boy was tugging on his mother's arm, trying to wake her from what seemed to have been a deep sleep. She never moved. Somehow, I knew that the boy's mother was dead. Who would take care of him? I can still hear his pleading voice.

"Mommy, get up! Mommy, get up!"

As we skirted through the streets of the city, I saw an endless number of lifeless bodies. These bodies would later be dumped into mass graves and burned. These were the sights and sounds of war. These would be the sights and sounds of a little girl growing up in the countryside of Iran.

After what seemed like several hours of running, we finally reached our home. We were glad to see that my brother and baby sister were safe and unharmed. The power of the entire city had been knocked out. The safest place to exist and stay alive during the bombings was underground in our basement, where we stayed for six days with no food or water as the bombings continued. We were hungry, we were tired, and we were very afraid . . . but we were alive.

It would be 30 days before my dad made it home. I was so happy to see him that I cried and laughed, and cried some more until I fell asleep. That night we rejoiced to know that we had all survived thus far.

While living with my family in our basement, I began to have feelings of responsibility. It was the kind of responsibility usually reserved for adults. The little boy on the side of the road was constantly in my thoughts. His dirty, tear-stained face and his pleading, tormented voice haunted me. If anything happened to my parents, I would take care of my brother and sister. I would be responsible.

I believe that everyone is born with a journey and a purpose in life. It is that purpose that gives ultimate meaning and must be pursued. The beginning of my journey was to pass through that stage of my life to strengthen me for what was to come. My journey demanded that I be strong enough to travel unchartered waters. My journey and my purpose required me to grow up to be a strong woman, an independent woman, and a victorious woman.

Roya Masaebi at Seven Years Old

A seven-year-old girl in Iran has little for which to dream. Dreams are for soldiers, politicians, and the men of Iran. My small bedroom was covered with pictures of the universe. The galaxies with its millions of stars somehow intrigued me. I sometimes sat for hours and looked at and got lost in my pictures. Pictures of Michael Jackson and Tina Turner assured me that there was a world beyond the borders of my country. The moon and stars were so far away, yet I could see them. I never questioned their existence or their reality. It was comforting to know that there was a reality beyond bombs, dead bodies, and crying babies on the side of country roads.

I could imagine living in America, going to an American college, and living a life of my own choosing. I refused to question this reality. I have always been a dreamer, and these were the things that my dreams were made of. My mother occasionally impatiently listened to my hopeless ramblings.

"I will leave Iran. One day, I will live in America. You will see. I will graduate from an American university. I will have my own business."

Most of my family laughed at me. I didn't care. When I closed my eyes, I could see a future beyond my small room. It was a future filled with unlimited possibilities. Like the galaxies, it was far away, but I could see it, and it was my reality.

I was in the third grade when I decided that I must learn to speak English. I wanted to be able to understand American music and what Michael Jackson and Tina Turner were singing about. Even as a child, I somehow knew that if my dreams were to come true, that I must learn about writing, reading, and understanding the language of my destiny. My dreams included going to America and graduating from an American college.

I was in the fourth grade when my dreams began to have feet. The journey began to unfold and I would never be the same. Whenever one experiences real growth, it is difficult to ever again feel comfortable in going back to a pre-growth condition.

I continued to talk to the universe and to the stars every night from inside of my heart, but I dared not tell anybody about my thoughts and my dreams. I knew that my family would not understand my need to talk to the universe. My family would have thought me to be insane and laughed at their little girl who had dreams of America, fueled by conversations with the universe.

One summer evening when I was in the fifth grade, a simple event happened to shed light and hope on my dreams. Someone was ringing our doorbell. It was one of my cousins with his brother in-law. My cousin was an animal doctor and professor at Tehran University. The two had come from Tehran to visit my family.

My cousin's brother in-law was just coming back from America, where he graduated from an American university. His parents sent him to America right after he finished high school. His dad was very rich and it was very important to his dad for all of his kids to have the best education. His name was Mehdi and he could hardly speak Farsi, but he was fluent at speaking the language of my dreams.

Hearing this man speak the language of America, and knowing that he had graduated from an American university had a profound impact on me. I could feel that somehow I was getting closer to my dreams. If this man could do it, I could too. The universe was calling me.

Sometimes reality can be a hard truth. The reality of my situation was that my father, while a great provider, was not a rich man. My reality included living in a country where my very existence was at constant risk. My most important reality was that not only did my father not believe in my dreams, he refused to see them as even being appropriate.

Little Iranian girls did not have the same opportunities as Iranian boys. In spite of my reality, the universe never stopped speaking to me. I would find a way. My dreams would come true. Seeing Mehdi gave me hope about my future.

When Mehdi saw how committed I was to learning English and how I dreamed about America, he said to me, "You are a very smart young girl and a hard worker. I don't see any reason why your dreams should not come true."

He told me that he would love to teach me English and that he would make me ready for the sixth grade, where students had the option of taking English as a foreign language. He told me that when I started classes, he would make sure that I would be ahead of my class.

The most important thing he told me was, "YOU WILL GO TO AMERICA ONE DAY. I CAN SEE THAT."

Finally, someone believed in me and was willing to help.

Chapter Two
Dying While Still Alive

Iranian women are taught at an early age to submit. Even the most fundamental decisions are left to the arbitrary ways, whims, and wants of men. Who you talk to, when you can go out to play, or even when you may eat are decisions that are dictated by the men of Iran. The male dominated culture greatly diminishes the aspirations of little Iranian girls. In this world, women grow up to be objects of pleasure or disposable laborers in a world made for and by domineering men. In Iran, one's ability to dream or to become is based not on ability, but on gender.

At the age of fifteen, while in the ninth grade, my parents forced me into a marriage that I did not want. I cried, yelled, and screamed that I did not want to be married. I could not understand why my parents would do such a thing to me. My mother, who was the one behind the decision, was not willing or able to hear my pleas. I rebelled, argued, and pleaded to my mother, but her mind was set.

Maybe my dreams were just the whimsical fantasies of a little girl, but I would rather die than let my parents so casually throw them away. I tried to commit suicide. I took as many pills as I could find. My only mistake was taking them while still in my house. Before the pills could have the desired effect, I was rushed to the hospital and my life, if not my dreams, was saved.

Maybe the universe had not given up on me. Maybe God did not want me to die. Maybe the stars were watching over me, and yet I could feel my hope slowly disappearing as my dreams faded under the shadow of my impending marriage.

I knew that if I got married there would be no chance for my dreams. I knew that if I got married I would be a slave, forced to have this stranger's babies, and have absolutely no rights as a human being. In Iran, when a woman gets married she is seen as being the property of her husband. Married women do not have rights. They only have multiple and non-ending duties and responsibilities. I knew that my husband would never let me go anywhere, especially to live in another country. Maybe the universe was watching over me, but its voice had become silent.

I was a child when the war started, and I never got to enjoy my life as a child. As soon as I wanted to enjoy a new place, we had to run away again from the constant bombings. From age seven to fifteen, my only reason to keep living had been my dream of going to America and one day having the freedom to live life as a human.

The marriage was a continuation of a childhood destined for misery and grief. Maybe my dreams were a cruel joke of the gods. I felt that my heart might literally stop at any time. I could not breathe. Something heavy was on my chest and everything turned to black in my life. I hated my parents. I especially hated my mom, because she was the one who turned off all my hopes in my life.

The day of my marriage, before I told him yes I said to him, "I promise and I swear to God that no matter how long I am married to you, I will leave you one day, because I don't love you and I have to follow my dreams."

I said yes to him, but by saying yes to this man that I absolutely hated, I was walking into a hell with no hope of truly living anymore.

There are few things in life that are worse than dying while you are still alive. The day of my marriage was the day that all laughter ceased to be a possibility in my life. My hopes and dreams were diminished to merely trying to avoid the horrors that became a part of my daily existence.

I am convinced that my husband was mentally ill. Every day there was a different reason for him to mercilessly beat me. If he could find no reason, he was certainly capable of making up one. My life was a living hell. My husband became obsessed with finding out what man had stolen the love that I would not give to him. Whenever he left the house, I had temporary peace, because the physical and emotional abuse would at least temporarily stop. A sixteen year old girl should not have to live like that.

I often sat paralyzed listening for clicks of the door handle, hoping that somehow, some catastrophe would befall my demented husband and keep him from returning home. My teenage years consisted of the horror of war in the outside world, and the horror of marriage inside of my home. Broken arms, blackened eyes, being doused with gasoline, regularly being shocked with an electric cow prod, and daily fearing for my life were reasons enough to one day leave this man.

The beatings were accompanied by screaming interrogations. "Who is he?" "Do you think I'm stupid?" "Do you think that I don't know what you are doing?"

There was no other man. There were only my dreams of a better life, and they were gradually fading. My goal was to finish beauty school, get my license, and make enough money to finance my escape from the hell that was my life. My dreams, though weakened by the reality of my daily existence, never completely disappeared.

Much to my surprise, I was allowed to go to night classes. The prospect of me being able to earn an income was appealing to my drug dealing husband. I occasionally continued to find moments where I could talk to the universe. I asked the universe to help me to live and not die. I asked the universe to help me find a way. Each beating intensified my desire to not let my dreams die and I with them.

I worked very hard and I saved my money. I built one of the best and most famous hair salons in my town. I opened up a beauty school and it also became successful. I found that I had a flare for business. Meanwhile, I was doing my research and developing a network of important people I needed to know to help me leave the land that had become my nightmare.

It took me seven years of saving, networking and researching, but I worked tirelessly. During that time, I was blessed with two beautiful little boys. They would now have to be a part of my dream. I was sixteen years old when I had my first child, Arash, and I was eighteen years old when I had my second child, Arman.

Dreams don't miraculously come true because we dream them. Dreams can, however, come true when we put feet and arms to them. Dreams can come true when we plan, and work, and struggle, and remain committed to that which we dare to dream. I continued to secretly save and plot and plan. I continued to dream.

In Iran, mistakes can cost you your life, but I could not let go of my dreams. I was committed to having a life of more. I put feet, arms, work, and struggle to my dreams. At the risk of death, I would make my dreams come true. It was not the way I had originally planned my life, but sometimes life just happens and we deal with where we are, not where we desire to be.

Chapter Three
Leaving Iran, Going to Germany

In the summer of 1996, when I was about twenty-three years old, I arrived at the airport to leave Iran, headed for Germany with my two boys. They were five and six years old. My years of saving, planning, networking, and plotting led me to that moment. I was very happy, because I was going to finally experience freedom. I would be free to pursue my dreams. I would be free from my abusive husband, the sounds and sights of war, and a repressive life. I, however, did not focus on what I was running from. I was too excited about what I was running to.

On the other hand, I was very much afraid of what was to come. What if something happened and the government officials at the airport decided to stop me? My heart was beating out of my chest. Every second seemed to be an eternity. I could not tell my boys where we were going for fear that they might be asked and say the wrong thing.

They continually asked me, "Where are we going, Mommy. Where are we going?"

I told them that we were going to northern Iran for vacation.

We arrived to the airport at three o'clock in the morning for check-in. I felt like I was having a heart attack every minute. It seemed that every official in the airport was watching me. I was trying to appear calm, but my heart struggled to beat within my chest. My pulse was racing and my clothes were drenched with the soaking perspiration caused by my almost painful nervousness.

I knew the risk of what I was trying to do. If I were to be caught smuggling my children out of the country with illegal passports, my life would come to a quick and certain end. The only thing I could do was pray and talk to the stars and the universe. For some reason I could feel they were listening to me.

When we were finally allowed to board the airplane, I breathed a deep sigh of relief. I was now a little bit more at ease. It seemed that the hardest part of the journey had been successfully completed. My boys were happy to be going on vacation. They had no idea of how permanent their vacation would be.

The plane slowly lifted from Iranian soil and eventually from Iranian airspace. I believe Dr. Martin Luther King Jr., the civil rights leader, said it best: "Free at last, free at last, thank God almighty, we're free at last."

We were on that airplane for eight hours. I didn't care. The plane eventually landed in Paris, France. Once we landed, I immediately removed my head scarf. Several other Iranian women nervously stared at me, but soon found the courage to remove their scarves as well. We all smiled with the knowledge that we were free to bare our hair to the world.

It may have been my newfound freedom, or maybe it was the novelty of my situation, but I had never before breathed such pure air.

This was my first experience of life outside of Iran, and I wanted to inhale every second of it.

The city of Paris was the most beautiful sight that I had ever seen. The sky seemed to be bluer, the grass seemed to be greener, and I was convinced that the trees were taller. The birds seemed to sing in harmony as they welcomed us to a new world. My kids were tired and hungry, and I began to worry about what would happen next.

The boys began to question where we were. They, no doubt, noticed that everyone was speaking an unfamiliar language and wearing unfamiliar clothes. The signs and sights of the Paris airport were strange and foreign to them. I needed to return to management mode and figure out what we must do next.

I finally informed my kids about the realities of our situation. Much to my surprise and relief, they were excited to be in a new country. While I knew that they did not fully grasp the seriousness of our situation, I was glad that they were momentarily happy.

The sister-in-law of our smuggler was waiting for us outside the airport. Before meeting her, I exchanged my American dollars to the currency of my final destination. The boys and I were soon headed to Germany. I had paid her brother $15,000.00, but this woman wanted more. I gave her the remainder of the money she said I owed her brother for safe passage out of Iran, and then purchased train tickets, which soon allowed us to arrive in Bonn, Germany. Had I known what the future held, I would have been hesitant to continue.

It was about 12:30 AM when we got to Bonn. I had arranged to meet a couple of friends who had already escaped from Iran. They picked us up from the train station and took us to their house where we stayed for the next few days. My friends then dropped me off in front of the police station where I walked in with my children and reported myself as a refugee. As I was walking into the police station and waiting to be processed, I saw another Iranian young man— maybe around my age—who was also waiting to be called. We started to talk and we quickly became friends.

It took several hours of paperwork, waiting, and more paperwork before we were officially welcomed to the country of Germany. We were then transferred to a temporary location where we stayed for the next three weeks. The temporary place the police took us was inside a big boat, like a cruise ship, on the Rhine River in Koln Germany. I decided to take my kids out to see the city with my Iranian friend I had just met in the police station.

The city was beautiful and amazing. I had never been in a country other than Iran, and was amazed to gaze on the differences in my new surroundings. The buildings, streets, the food, the language and signs all gave evidence of being in a different world.

I was happy and yet simultaneously depressed. I was happy because of my newfound independence and freedom. I was happy to feel that I was getting closer to my dreams, and I was proud of myself for what I had accomplished in getting myself and my children out of Iran.

I was depressed because I was worried about the uncertainty of what would happen next. I did not know where we would be sent, and realized that I had no power to affect my immediate destiny. Some refugees were saying that if you didn't have family to sponsor you, the police would send you anywhere or to any city where they might have an opening. I heard horror stories about some of these sites; stories about the sites being filled with criminals, child molesters, murderers, and rapists. These thoughts had me worried and periodically depressed.

We lived in the boat for about two weeks. We were then sent to a city in the south of Germany called Zinndorf. Zinndorf was a very small and old city located in the state of Nurnberg. Zinndorf was one of the infamous cities where Hitler killed countless numbers of the Jewish people by throwing them in gas ovens. These atrocities took place in the buildings right in back of where we had been sent.

I came to know that we had been sent to a place that had been used as a refugee camp for the Jews during World War II. It was the place where the German government now temporarily kept refugees until they could be interviewed and checked for any health issues.

The new place was like another prison to me. The entrance was continually guarded by two German police officers. The two officers guarded steel, locked gates at the entrance. The gates were bordered by long walls that housed the individual cell-like rooms to which we were assigned. I would come to see this place as hell on earth.

The constant smell of human waste and alcohol was accompanied by the periodic violent sounds of refugees fighting, women getting raped, and children crying out in sheer terror. I began to wonder if I would ever come out alive. I would have to find a way to survive. My God, what had I done?

I was constantly on guard for the safety of my children. The German government seemed to care very little for the lives of refugees. I asked myself, "Could this be the outcome of my dreams? Could this be what my life had come to?"

We were instructed to check in at the front office of the kitchen three times a day. We checked in early morning, noon, and evening to get food. If for any reason we failed to show up, we were not allowed to eat. Two times a week we were also given boxes that contained various snacks.

Refugee camps are not for the weak or faint of heart. The camp consisted of people from different races, nationalities, religions, and cultures. At night, different groups got together to drink and party until the night slowly turned to day. Sometimes the men got drunk and fought each other. Other times the combination of alcohol and dancing led to sexual situations and public displays of uncivilized behavior. This was the place of my newfound freedom.

We were encouraged to never leave the camp, but if we did, we had to be back before midnight. Failure to follow these instructions could lead to, at worst, possible deportation or the loss of identification cards, which were necessary to move throughout the city. My sons and I stayed at Zinndorf for two and a half months.

After completing a series of interviews and health checks, we were eventually transferred to the city of Schwabach. Schwabach was about one hour away from Zinndorf. We arrived at the camp around noon. The distance in space from Zinndorf did not come with a change of living conditions. If anything, our living conditions declined into a deeper hell. The Schwabach camp also had a dirty history. It had previously been used to house American prisoners of war.

My sons and I walked through the camp hoping to find other refugees from Iran. We found none. The camp consisted of refugees from Albania, Russia, and Yugoslavia.

As I was walking through the camp with my sons, a man came up to me and started speaking to me in German. He was the manager of the residential building. They called him the House Master. He assigned us a room and provided the essentials for us to immediately survive. The room was cold, dirty and small, but it was ours. I was not happy and very uncomfortable there, but I had no choice. I had to accept it.

I started to clean the room and get some food and a bath ready for the boys. I was young and pretty, and many of the men in the camp were after me. Being a single mom with two children in such a place was a daunting task. I was continually in a mental state of protecting myself and my children from the harshness of the environment. The men of the camp sometimes looked at us as if we were easy prey. I was determined to not let that be the case.

The first night I could not sleep at all. At night the camp became a large party of drunken debauchery. The refugees were inviting their friends to their rooms, getting drunk, and having sex. They were loud, frequently fought, and started hitting each other or throwing heavy furniture out of their windows. I was living in a jungle. We were forced to endure in that horrible place for two years.

Morning to night, each day became a struggle to survive. I made sure to keep our little area clean. I also cleaned the entire first floor every day. I did not want my boys to be sick from all the trash some of the other refugees were throwing out of their windows onto the residential grounds. It sometimes smelled as if we were living in the center of a sewage treatment dump.

After three months in the camp, I heard a rumor that other Iranian families would be transferred to our camp. I was very happy that I might have people from my country at the camp. At least I would not feel alone anymore.

I started to go to school to learn the German language. I stayed in Germany for almost five years. My ability to speak German eventually became strong enough to allow me to be an interrupter for other Iranian families. I enjoyed helping other Iranians through the burdensome processes of being a refugee.

I began to teach my boys the German language. When they started school, they were able to speak both Farsi, their native language, and German fluently.

Every Tuesday and Thursday, all the refugees were given a box of food. The boxes were provided between 9:00 AM to 12:00 PM. The boxes contained meat, chicken, yogurt, beans, chocolate, a soft drink, and various other food items. I was getting three adult boxes and two children's boxes. The food was not bad, and it was usually more than enough.

On the first day of each month, I went to the downtown refugee office to get money. I was getting 80 Marks for myself and 80 Marks for my children. Each child was allotted 40 Marks. The money, however, was not enough. By the end of the first day of the month, the money would be nearly gone. That was the situation for all the refugees in our camp.

In the north state of Germany, refugees had a better life situation. They were living in individual apartments and getting over 500 Marks for each person in the family. I later came to understand that I had been transferred to one of the worst and troubled states in Germany. Nobody wanted to live there in that refugee camp.

The first day that I entered the camp I tried to leave the city of Schwabach. It was not for me and I knew it. My kids and I deserved better. I wanted to be transferred to the city of Nuremberg, because I knew many of my people were there. Getting out of Iran had been one of the biggest steps in my life. I thought that when I left Iran that all of my problems would be solved, but that wasn't the case. My life's journey of fighting to realize my dreams had just begun. I was determined to fight. I was determined to win.

A German social worker came to our camp twice a week for about four hours. She was given office space to address the many concerns of refugees within the camp. Refugees stood outside of her office for hours to talk to her about any problems they had. She was a genuinely nice lady and would do anything that she could to help. There were certainly enough serious issues to keep this woman busy. I, for one, was constantly seeking advice and assistance from her.

I told her of the troubles of keeping me and my sons safe in the camp. Every week I made it my business for her to make me her business. I was constantly asking her to help me find a way to be transferred to the Nuremberg camp.

Being granted approval to move to a different camp or city wasn't easy. The German government was not interested in responding to the arbitrary whims of its refugee population. In order to be granted permission to move, I would have to show proof of some medical or mental illness. The stress of my situation had created what might be my way out of that hell hole. I developed debilitating migraine headaches, which sometimes drove me to collapse into a fetal position in the corner of my room.

I was determined that the social worker would hear me. Every day she was scheduled to come to the camp, I made it my business to see her. There were times when she would say that she could not see me, but no was not an acceptable answer.

After one and half years of listening to my plight, the social worker finally decided to help me with the necessary documentation to move to Nuremberg. In fact, it was her idea to use my migraine headaches as the medical reason for my move. She decided to take me to one of the Nuremburg hospitals to stay there for an overnight observation. The doctor needed to confirm that my migraine headaches required a different environment than the raucous, sometimes violent Schwabach camp.

Sometimes when something good is finally within grasp, life has a way of moving the finish line a little farther away. When the social worker took me to the hospital in Nuremburg, she was told that the hospital didn't have any empty rooms. Determined to help me, she took me to a different hospital, maybe forty-five minutes from our camp. The next words that came out of this woman soon proved to be untrue, and the beginning of a new nightmare.

Chapter Four

A New Nightmare

"If you can stay here for a couple of days, I can get a letter from the doctor that will enable you to move from Schwabach," the social worker told me. "Don't worry about your kids. I know a very good German family. They will take care of your children until you come back."

I trusted her. I needed this to happen. I needed it to happen for my boys. I needed it to happen for me.

As I walked into the hospital, I felt that something was different. I didn't know exactly why I felt that way, but I almost immediately felt like a dark heaviness was surrounding me. There was something definitely different about it.

I paused in the hospital lobby as my eyes took inventory of the cold, almost prison-like environment. There were bars on the windows. Several guards in white uniforms roamed the lobby. It did not look like any hospital that I had ever seen.

I got a sick feeling in the pit of my stomach. I was afraid, but I didn't know why. My heart was beating out of my chest and my palms were sweaty. My stomach felt like I was at the top of a rollercoaster. Almost involuntarily I blurted out, "I don't want to stay here!"

"I am sorry, but you don't have any choice," the social worker said. "We don't have any other hospitals close to us. This is the only hospital that has an empty room. I have already checked. The other hospitals in the region are all referring us here. Either you have to stay here for few days, or go back to Schwabach with no chance of ever moving from the camp."

She did my paperwork and left me at the hospital. I was trapped. There was no way out of my situation. She said that after my observation she would come back for me. Without fully understanding why, I started to cry. My face stayed wet with the warmth of my tears throughout the night.

I soon found out why I had such an uneasy feeling walking into that place. The hospital was located in the town called Ansbach. It was just south of Nuremburg. The name of the hospital, Bezirksklinkum, was familiar to me.

Oh my God! I thought as soon as I recalled having heard about the hospital.

It was the same hospital that one of my refugee friends had told me about. Bezirksklinkum was a hospital for the mentally insane. People sent to Bezirksklinkum were never seen again. It was rumored that the only way out was to be carried out in a pine box. What was happening to my dreams? Why were they doing this to me? What would happen to my boys?

I asked if I could use the phone and was allowed to do so. I called my refugee friend and told him the entire story. The fear and anxiety in his voice only magnified my own fears.

In the morning I went to the head doctor's office to ask that I be released. He smiled before telling me that releasing me was not an immediate possibility. I was so scared. I needed to see my children. What was happening to them?

My friend had told me that no matter what, I must not take any medication given to me. He advised me to hold the medication under my tongue and drink the water the nurse gives me.

"If you take their medicine," he had warned me, "your brain will be damaged and they will be able to keep you. Make a sound like you are swallowing the medication."

He instructed me to throw the medicine in the toilet and flush it as soon as the attendant left the room. I followed his advice. I did not want to die in that God forsaken place. My friend promised to do whatever he could to get me out of my hell.

It was my second day at the hospital, but I felt that I had been there for a hundred years. The only thing I could do was to cry and pray. I was holding my kids' picture every minute, talking to them and crying for them. I missed my children so much. I prayed that God would protect them in my absence.

In the meantime, my children were with the German family the social worker had placed them with. With the help of my friend, it took about two weeks until I got out of Bezirksklinkum. How could I have ended up in a place worse than the camp that I so desperately needed to escape from?

Upon my release, the social worker took me to pick up my children from their assigned German family. I cannot explain the feeling I had in that moment. My boys were hanging down off of my neck, and we just kept kissing each other. They were so happy and scared at the same time.

Arash and Arman in Germany

We started talking. I asked them what happened to them in the last two weeks. They told me of their experience with the German family. It was not only me that had been having a hard time; my kids had been in their own two weeks of hell. My kids had been separated from each other, unable to talk to or play with each other. They had unfortunately, been introduced to the racist culture of Germany.

They were in a constant state of being punished. They missed each other terribly. They were not allowed to speak to each other, and if they were caught doing so, they were punished severely. Yet in the middle of the night they would often sneak to each other's room to talk and pray to be reconnected with me.

They shared with me how they were afraid that they would never again see me. They came up with the idea that if they had some money, they might be able to get me out of the hospital. One day when the German couple left the house, my kids went to the basement to play and saw 15 Marks on the table. The couple had put the money there to test my kids. Unaware of the trap, the boys decided to take the money to help me get out of the hospital.

The couple had placed hidden cameras throughout the house. When the couple arrived back home, they immediately saw that the money was missing and began to interrogate the boys. They told the boys that they would be sent to jail and that they would never again see me. The boys were trembling with fear as they confessed to taking the money to get me out of the hospital.

The couple called the social worker to have her report my sons to the police as juvenile thieves. Fortunately, they reached the same social worker that had placed me in the hospital. This lady decided to not report my kids. Her decision kept my boys out of the German juvenile criminal system, and for that I will forever be grateful.

Chapter Five
Moving to Nuremburg

It was September 1997 when we moved to a very nice neighborhood just north of Nuremburg. It took me almost one week to settle down and enroll my kids into the Nuremburg School. Our life was the same; nothing changed except being in a new place and new city. The rules and regulations for refugees were the same. We were not to leave the town, we were not permitted to work, and we were forced to live off of the food boxes two times a week; every Tuesday and Thursday from 9:00 AM to 12:00 PM. We received three adult food boxes and two kid boxes, which was okay, but still was not everything we needed. The rule remained the same that if I did not make it on time to get the boxes, I lost all the food, which never happened.

I forgot to mention that on day one when I entered Germany, I started doing hair for many of the women refugees in every camp I was assigned to. I was making enough money to help me to buy some extra things that my children needed.

The new camp I moved to in Nuremburg was a four-story building that included a basement. I was located on the last floor, which was the fourth floor. There seemed to be hundreds of stairs to climb. On food box day, I had to make several trips from the fourth floor to the basement, which is where the food boxes were distributed. I had to carry all the boxes to my room by the end of the day. I was in lots of back pain, but I had no complaints because I was grateful to have a better place to live.

On the same floor I was on, there were two Russian families. One of them was a couple with no children. The other family was a couple with two children. On the third floor were two single women from the country of Eritrea. The two single women weren't there much. They stayed at their German boyfriends' houses a lot.

On the second floor resided two Iranian families. One was a single mom with two boys. She married an Iranian man just to get German citizenship. She was living in that guy's house, but also kept her room at the camp. She didn't want to lose her benefits as a refugee. Basically, she was taking advantage of the German government.

The other family on the second floor was another single mom in her 50s. She was there with her adult daughter. Both were trouble. They'd each been with so many men; a different man almost each day. The mom had even had a relationship with the camp refugee manager just to get more stuff and to be kept on the first floor because that floor was the best area in the building. The first floor was used as storage for the food and supplies.

The mom and the manager could have gone to jail if they had been found out. It was illegal and against the rules for them to have a relationship.

The mother and daughter never liked me. I had seen the mother when she was kissing the building manager. Since then, she and her daughter were always looking to fight with me. I tried to stay away from both of them because they were wild, loud, and dangerous.

Even though the new place was much better than any previous camp, there were still lots of issues I had to face.

In order to stay in Germany, I needed to receive a passport issued by the German government. The German officials had been made to look foolish by too many Iranians who claimed political hardship, only to regularly go back to Iran to visit family and friends. I needed to prove that my life would be endangered if refugee status was not granted. I found this difficult to do. It was, in fact, my reality. But it was not enough. Three times the court denied my requests for refugee status. I was then identified as being returnable to Iran. For me, it was a death sentence.

I was ordered to go to the governmental offices to take the pictures necessary to give me an Iranian passport so that I could be sent back to Iran. How could they do this? Did they not understand? My life was in their hands. I would fight them. If it cost me my life, I was determined to not die on Iranian soil.

The Iranian government required that passport pictures of Iranian women show the women with their heads covered. That would be my way out. Only over my dead body would I allow that picture to be taken.

On November 3, 1999, I had been sleeping in my room. It was not a peaceful sleep, as every minute was now filled with the anticipation of fighting for my life. Today would be the day.

"Get up!" I was awakened by the harsh sound of two huge, angry German officers. I was told to get a scarf and cover my head. "I do not have one," I fearfully protested. "We will find one for you."

I was dragged from my room. Once in the police station, I was slammed into a chair and ordered to cover my hair. Other officers came to join the fight. My arms were pinned behind my back as officers tried to force a scarf over my head. I turned my head. I needed to fight. I was determined, if necessary, to die in the struggle.

Somehow, in the midst of the struggle, I could see the posters on my wall from my childhood. In this moment of horrible violence, I could hear the universe imploring me to keep fighting. This would be the moment that determined if my dreams would die and I with them.

After thirty minutes of constant fighting with the six police officers, my face was bruised. My left shoulder was slightly separated. My neck was discolored by bruises from the uncaring police hands and arms. My head was throbbing and the officers had what they believed to be an acceptable photograph. I was dropped off at my apartment and ordered to wait for further notice of deportation. I would now have a life of hiding.

The next four months consisted of darkness. There was no light. There was no sun. My children did not understand the constant need of silence. How could I explain why they could not play in the warmth of the sun?

The Iranian community was somehow made aware of my situation. A twenty-four year old woman with two children was a sympathetic figure with whom people could relate. Much to my surprise, people took to the streets of Germany to protest my plight. I was not alone. My case soon garnered international attention. I received letters from American lawyers saying that they would protect me. People from places that I had never seen were offering to fight with me. They were offering to fight for me.

In Iran, I had never heard of the phrase "human rights." It was a phrase that I would come to love. The struggle to be free took much longer than I imagined. It would be many years filled with midnight tears and daytime horrors before I left German soil. In the midst of darkness, it was hard to see the light, but freedom eventually came.

Chapter Six

Going to America

August 18, 2000, my mind was frozen, yet it was racing. The flight attendant was helping everyone to put their baggage in the overhead bins. My two sons were eight and nine years old. While the magnitude of the situation escaped these unsuspecting children, the boys had an unexplained sense of anticipation. As the plane began its takeoff, my heart felt like it was going to explode. I had said goodbye to Iran, and I was now saying goodbye to Germany. Soon I would realize the dream that occupied my childhood. Soon I would be on American soil.

As the plane arrived over American soil, I saw the city of New York. I remember seeing the city in the movies, but now I was seeing it in real life . . . and it was amazing. The Statue of Liberty was holding up her torch to light my way into the wonderful land of America. It was the most beautiful and delightful feeling I ever had in my life. My heart was beating so fast that I became afraid I might have a heart attack!

After all these years, I still cannot describe that most marvelous feeling. All of the horrors and nightmares of my life dimmed in the glory of that moment. There would be other challenges and obstacles to overcome, but I could once again talk to the universe.

In June of 2006, I proudly became a citizen of the United States of America. On September of 2011, I proudly walked across the graduation stage of Columbus State Community College to receive an Associate Degree in Business Management. I wanted so badly to be able to hug the little seven year old Iranian girl with the unrealistic dreams. I wanted to tell the fifteen year old married Roya that morning always follows the night.

After the ceremony, I looked in the mirror and cried, but it was a happy cry. It was a cry that washed away the pain of my past and ushered in the hopes of my tomorrow. I wanted to shout to the world that dreams do indeed come true.

Roya with Professor Barksdale at Graduation

On September 21, 2014, I walked across the stage of Franklin University to receive a Bachelor of Science degree in Business Administration. While I have traveled many miles and experienced many triumphs and failures, the best is yet to come. I am currently working toward my master's degree, and there will soon be a book, and perhaps a movie, about my story. I can still see the stars, and the universe is still quietly speaking to me. It is good to know that dreams do come true, because I can't seem to stop having them.

In the fourteen years of my journey on American soil, Michael Jackson has passed away, and Tina Turner no longer lives in the United States. The moon and the stars, however, are still shining brightly in the midnight sky, and I still occasionally gaze at them. The universe is still speaking.

Many books have been written about dreams. Some say that nocturnal dreams are merely reflections of what resides in our subconscious mind. Others declare that the dreams we have during our sleep are simply the product of a bad night time diet. These are not the types of dreams which are the subject of this truth. The subject of my truth is that when you put legs, arms, and a will that refuses to give up to your dreams, your dreams—and my dreams—can come true.

Part II

"I Started From the Bottom"

(James Witherspoon's Story)

Chapter One
No Way Out

I grew up in Detroit, Michigan in the nineteen seventies. At the time it was a prosperous town with the automotive industry in full swing; hence the nickname Motor City. It was rumored that my dad hitchhiked in the middle of winter from Cincinnati, Ohio to Detroit to get a job at Uniroyal tire plant while I was still in my mother's stomach. My father was a big man in stature; six feet and one inch tall, medium build, baby face, and clean-cut. If you had seen him out and about, you would have considered him a model citizen. But nobody knew the secrets that went on behind closed doors.

He was a loving, caring man . . . as long as he didn't have any alcohol or drugs in his system. When he did, he was a selfish, self-centered bastard.

A typical night in my house, whether it was a school night or the weekend, went like this: I would be awakened by loud music. It was usually Bob Seager's "Turn the Page" blasting out of the old box stereo that was sitting on four legs with the flip up tops that displayed the eight track player and the LP turn tables. Records were usually all over the floor, some in the sleeves and some just lying around. It was the seventies and my father made decent money for that time, but he drank a lot of it up and gambled more of it away.

Our furniture was nice, so to speak. Placed around our living room was a dark brown sofa and loveseat made out of this corduroy-like material. There was also a coffee table and two end tables made of light brown oak wood. A fish tank was set up against one wall in the living room. It had a boa constrictor and a couple of mice running around in it just waiting to be eaten. My dad would get drunk and feed the snake and watch it eat the mice. He considered that a good time.

My dad's friends were shady looking characters. By that I mean they looked like they hadn't showered in days. They had long hair, rough beards, and tattoos. All his friends looked like this. Although he hung out with them, he never looked like he fit in, but always appeared to be the leader of the group.

One evening in particular I rolled over in my bed, awakened by the loud music. I wiped my eyes, got up, opened my bedroom door, and went to use the bathroom. When I stepped out of the room, my father and three of his friends were in the living room. I looked around, and the coffee table was full of pills and a large amount of white powder. I didn't know at the time, but later learned that it was cocaine. Cans were all over the floor and table. Clouds of smoke with a funny odor filled the room. I later learned that was a result of my dad and his buddies smoking marijuana.

Before I could make it to the bathroom, my father saw me and got angry.

"Get back in your room!" he yelled at me.

One of his friends laughed, soon after offering me a beer. I declined and went back in my room, frightened and still having to use the bathroom.

I lay there in my bed scared to death listening to the music. There was laughter and talk of women and sexual escapades. These were things that a nine year old shouldn't see or hear.

I looked over at my brother to see that he'd slept through all this noise and commotion. I lay there frozen until I finally fell back asleep. There are instances when time freezes and the pain of the moment is left to torture the recipient of the infliction. A child is not emotionally or physically equipped to deal with such situations, but I was forced to.

I lay there staring at the ceiling, wishing that I was somewhere else. I didn't know where I wanted to be, I just knew that anywhere else would have been an improvement. After what must have been three hours, I got up and walked out of the room across the hall to my mother and fathers' bedroom door. I could hear struggling and yelling. My mother was yelling for my father to stop whatever it was he was doing.

"You're hurting me! Please stop!"

I was scared to death. My hands were shaking and trembling while I was crying. As I heard my father yelling, I gathered all the courage that I had in my nine year old body and said as loud as the fear would let me, "Mom, you okay?"

I then heard a loud voice that sounded like a lion's roar.

"Get back in your room before I beat that ass!"

I ran into my room and jumped into my bed. I pulled the covers over my head, trembling in fear until I fell asleep, drowning out the screams of terror from the other room.

This was the first time in my life that I felt powerless. I had no ability to fix the situation that I was in. I was completely at the mercy of a dysfunctional parent. The man that I should have been able to look up to was the cause of my fear. A child should be able to receive love and support from their parents. My father obviously did not share this belief.

The next day my mom had a black eye and a broken arm. If I, at the young age of nine, were to look for protection, where could I look? The woman who couldn't protect herself, or the man who was willing to hurt the ones that he supposedly loved?

Chapter Two
Wrong Decisions Last a lifetime

My father decided to move the family to Cincinnati Ohio. In 1986, I graduated high school. Despite my father, I did fairly well. I promised myself throughout life that I would be nothing like him and would never drink alcohol. I didn't go to the graduation ceremonies. I celebrated with a few close friends and started to plan how to get as far away from home as possible. My grades were good enough to get me into The Ohio State University (OSU). As a family, we took a trip to visit the campus. I had orientation and they gave me a tour. I remember the campus being huge. There were so many people that I felt overwhelmed and frightened.

I had never been away from home before. The fear of the unknown and being on my own took away any confidence I might have had. When we got back to Cincinnati, I decided I didn't want to go to OSU. About that same time a recruiter from DeVry Institute of Technology in Columbus, Ohio called me and sold me on the idea of going there. The campus was smaller with far less people than OSU. I would still be away from home, but it seemed manageable to me. I worked at Kroger and saved all my money for the upcoming school year.

The day came when it was time for me to head off to college. The recruiter was picking me up from my home in Cincinnati and taking me to Columbus. He had my apartment already set up. I was more than ready to call myself a college student. I knew that I was starting a journey that would change the course of my life. My brother, who was two years younger than me, and my sister who was only eight, cried as if they were losing me forever. I held my sister and assured her that I would see her between quarters and during the holidays.

Right before I left, my father called me down to the basement, saying that he needed to talk to me. He told me to sit down. He then began to slowly pace as if he were trying to find his words. My father wasn't exactly a warm and sensitive guy that regularly engaged in father and son dialogue. I assumed that he was going to tell me not to flunk out of school or bring any babies home.

"Son, you're going to be in a strange city where you don't know nobody, and times could get rough." He then handed me two guns. "Always keep one by your bedside and always carry one wherever you go for protection."

I stared down at the guns as my heart began beating louder and harder. I'd never handled a gun in my life. I had seen guns around the house, but knew that touching one of them would have resulted in a severe beating. I wasn't sure how to load or use either of the guns, but I was afraid to ask for instructions. I was sure I could figure it out.

His last statement before I headed off to college was, "Son, if you ever pull a gun out, you better use it."

I was eighteen years old and this was my father's last piece of advice for me. In a strange way, I looked up to him in spite of the alcoholism and frequent abuse toward my mother. My father was a man's man.

The recruiter got there and we loaded up the car. I remember hugging my mom while she was sobbing with her head buried in my chest. Her first born son was heading off to college. In retrospect, I wonder if my leaving the house caused her to fear having one less witness in the house of her sometimes abusive life.

I got in the car with the recruiter and we headed for Columbus. Still to this day I'm sure he has no idea that I had a loaded .22 automatic pistol tucked in my belt.

I got dropped off in downtown Columbus in a one bedroom, furnished apartment, which consisted of outdated furniture, a refrigerator, and a small television. This was my home sweet home. It wasn't much, but it was mine and I could come and go as I pleased.

The college set me up with a job busting suds in the school cafeteria, and I attended classes at night. Nobody ever knew that at work, in class, or even on the bus ride home at night, I always carried my .22 automatic in my pants.

I was hanging out in the lobby/lounge at DeVry one day and ran into a good friend from Cincinnati named Tyrone. We got to talking about old times, and he told me that he lived in a condo with roommates and they had a bedroom available for rent. He said that if I wanted it, I could have it. All alone in a big city, the move sounded like a great idea. Breaking my current lease seemed little more than a small inconvenience.

The condo felt like a frat house and I loved my roommates. It felt like a great improvement from my original living arrangements.

One of my roommate's, Henz, was a tall Mexican gentleman with dark, curly hair and a mustache. He always dressed in designer clothes that never seemed to match. He was in his last few semesters at DeVry. This dude always had some kind of hustle going—selling clothes or mixtapes—to make ends meet.

My roommate, Mike, was a ladies man with women on opposite sides of town that took care of his every need. In a way, I admired his lifestyle. He didn't work, just hung out, partied, and every other day the women would take turns coming over and buying him clothes and food.

Tyrone was more of a street cat. He was fairly tall, medium build, and always had the latest fashions. Tyrone was an aspiring rapper and was really good at it. He was in his last semester at DeVry and was able to support his craft and his wardrobe from the money he earned working at UPS. I wasn't counting the hours he worked, but he seemed to always have a lot of money and he loved to drink beer.

At times I wasn't sure that I fit in with this group. They were more experienced, faster, and sharper than the sometimes quiet guy from the Natti.

One of the first few weekends in the condo, I can remember everyone getting ready for a party on the east side of town. Tyrone was going to the store and asked me if I wanted to ride along with him. I agreed and we were off. Hanging around Tyrone always made me feel a little cooler than I probably was.

When we got to the store, he was picking up forty ounce bottles of beer for him and the other guys. "Go ahead and get you one." He nodded toward the cooler that stored the beer.

I remember a feeling of embarrassment when I told him I didn't drink. He laughed and said, "Come on, man. Get you just one."

He didn't know my history. He didn't understand the hell that alcohol had caused my family. I couldn't find the words to describe my hesitancy. I stood in the middle of the store aisle looking at bottles and cans of alcohol, feeling that I was about to make a terrible decision.

I was so naive that I didn't know what to get. Back at home I had seen thousands of beer cans laying around the house, but didn't know what to grab from that cooler. So I grabbed a forty ounce bottle of Pink Champale.

I remember it like it was yesterday; the forty ounce bottle with the pink label, the condensation dripping off the bottle, even the liquid inside looked pink. It looked harmless. It was just a drink, right? What could it hurt? I had no idea at the time how much power that liquid really had and the impact it would soon have on my life.

Tyrone paid for the beer and it was a long ride home, even though the store was only ten minutes away from our condo. I felt a rush of anxiety come over me. I didn't want to become my father, but I wanted to stand strong in front of my friends and not be a punk.

I wanted to belong. When we got home, I took the beer into my room and put my clothes on to get ready for the party.

Staring at the bottle of beer, there was an inner fight going on inside my head. The devil was telling me to go ahead, it was just one drink, and to have a good time. My conscience was saying, "You don't need that to have fun. You don't want to turn out like your father do you?"

I walked over and grabbed hold of the bottle. I slowly turned the lid to open it. I can still hear the crackling noise as I twisted it to break free the lid. It was like the disease was already calling for me before it even touched my lips. I put the bottle to my lips and took the first drink of it. I remember thinking to myself, *this isn't so bad.*

I was totally unaware of a predisposition to alcohol addiction. It never occurred to me that the addictions of my father may have provided some genetic probability that this innocent introduction to alcohol would take me to a place where I didn't want to be.

It tasted good, and before long, I finished it up and felt different. I was always a shy kid, but now I was confident and outspoken. I always thought I was ugly, but now I didn't look so bad. This little bit of liquid gave me confidence and strength, and the fear of being the unaccepted oddball was gone. I WAS ALIVE and I liked the way it felt.

I could see why my daddy drank the stuff. I was transformed; new, whole, and fearless. I was ready for anything. They called it liquid courage and I was learning to appreciate its powers.

We all got ready and left for the party. Some other people came over, so we decided to take two cars. We stopped at the store and picked up some more beer and began drinking it in the car on the way to the party.

Tyrone was driving. I guess he had experience with drinking and driving, considering he drank all the time. Tyrone's drinking and driving was the only thing that I thought wasn't cool about him. I knew that it was irresponsible for him to put his life and the life of others at risk.

The music was blasting Public Enemy and everyone was trying to finish their beers before we got to the party. We pulled up to the house party and there were about fifteen people in the front yard chilling. I could hear the music blaring. Once out of the car and approaching the house, the smell of alcohol filled the air.

"I gotta piss real bad," Tyrone said. He ran down the yard and went behind a tree while we were all still standing there talking smack about each other. Time passed and I began to wonder what was taking Tyrone so long.

I was feeling the effects of the alcohol, but I didn't know what buzzed or drunk was yet, because this was my first experience. All I knew was that I felt invincible.

I started to walk down to check on Tyrone. As I got closer, I could see a man holding a gun on Tyrone. The adrenaline started to rush through me like I had just hit the mega millions lottery. I crept up real slow behind the guy with the gun on Tyrone and pulled out the

.22 my daddy had given me. I put it to the guy's head and told him to drop his gun. He dropped it and Tyrone zipped up his pants and yelled at me.

"Come on, man, let's go!"

At that instant, the words my daddy said to me rang in my head. "Son, if you pull it out, you better use it."

I didn't know what would happen if I didn't use it, but I knew that I had pulled it out. I knew that I couldn't back down after pointing the gun at this man's head.

The alcohol had me feeling powerful and fearless, and those words from my daddy, the toughest man I knew, rang in my head. Then without even a second thought, with a split second decision and the gun to his head, I pulled the trigger.

CLICK! CLICK!

Going Nowhere Fast

Chapter Three
The End is Near

Sometimes we are fortunate and life saves us from ourselves. I am not a convicted murderer today because the gun jammed. I decided to move back to Cincinnati. The next four years of my life were spent going in and out of relationships, schools, jobs, and living conditions. My drinking continued to intensify, and school, employment and relationships were held hostage to my addiction. I began to add various drugs to my lifestyle. I was chasing a feeling and didn't care what I did to get it. I began to emotionally abuse women and I found it difficult to stay in any relationship longer than a few months.

I was selfish, out of control, unwilling and perhaps unable to put the brakes on my self- destructive lifestyle. My life would be a life of addiction for a total of twenty two years. In that period I would father six children by three different women, lose countless jobs, and because of evictions or running from relationships, lived at a countless number of different addresses. My life had become a horror story, and unfortunately I had spread my horror to those who were unlucky enough to get too close to me.

Decembers in Cincinnati were often cold and dreary. The dreariness was just slightly offset by the lights and sounds of the Christmas season. It was a typical Saturday morning for me. I woke up with a hangover and went into the bathroom and threw up big globs of acid; my normal routine. I got sick every day for at least five years.

That was my body's way of rejecting the alcohol, but I had to have it to function in my life. The disease had taken over my mind.

Wiping my mouth, I headed to the refrigerator and grabbed my breakfast; a cold can of Milwaukee's Best Ice. Sitting alone at the kitchen table, I started to look around my one-bedroom apartment. I remember thinking, *I have finally found the hell I was headed for ever since I was eighteen years old.*

My mind state was always me against the world, and if you didn't like it, you could get out of my life. This morning was different though. The apartment was cold and it seemed smaller than usual. A man that used to have it all and no worries, I was now broken down to an apartment with just a TV, kitchen table and chairs, and a futon couch.

I had pushed all my friends away with my violent and unpredictable behavior that was a result of my drinking. When I drank, all bets were off. I did what I wanted when I wanted to do it. It didn't matter whose feelings got hurt, just as long as I got what I wanted. The monster I had become was a liar, a cheat, and a thief fueled by my alcoholism.

This particular morning my head was spinning, not from the hangover, but in a suicidal funk, filled with all types of dark thoughts. The last few nights I had given it a halfhearted cowardly try by trying to drink myself to death. Like that was really going to work. My tolerance was built up to a thirty-pack of beer a night, and usually a couple of shots of something. Then the thought hit me that changed my life forever.

I can't live with it and I can't live without it.

My life couldn't go on like this. I was fed up and at the end of my rope, but too much of a coward to kill myself. Then a friend called to check on me and to tell me about this church that was giving away free Christmas dinners. It was around eight o'clock in the morning and I was already drinking, so I told her I would pass. She kept on badgering me to go, so I finally agreed and got myself together as best I could. A man who once had three cars was now driving a friend's car on loan.

I jumped in the car and headed to Kentucky to the church in order to get my free Christmas dinner. Kentucky, although another state, wasn't but a quick drive from where I stayed in Cincinnati. I took a six-pack with me for the ride and was drinking all the way there.

Crazy thoughts raced through my mind the entire trip. Thoughts like whether I should just run the car into the guardrail and flip it over, killing myself. But I didn't want to total my friend's car. Thinking back on it now, that was my state of mind. I was more worried about a car than my own life. Ending it all would break the grip this disease had on me once and for all.

I made it to the church and the people there were really nice, despite the fact that I smelled like a brewery and hadn't showered in a couple days. They gave me a big Christmas dinner and even let me pick out some gifts for my kids, because I didn't have any presents for them. All of my money was going toward alcohol.

There was no way of knowing that what was about to happen would change my life forever.

As I was leaving and saying goodbye to everyone and thanking them for their hospitality, a woman came through the church door. We passed each other, locking eyes in the process.

"Hi." Her voice was soft and pleasant.

"Hello," I replied.

At that point she asked me a question that left me standing there confused and lost.

"Is there anything that I can help you with, or anything you need to tell me?" Her eyes were just as soft and pleasant as her voice, but her tone was knowing.

She knew. But how did she know? How did she know I had a problem that was making me want to take my own life? It couldn't have been the fact that my breath smelled like a brewery and I weighed about one-sixty and hadn't showered in days. They'd certainly seen my kind come and go.

I wondered if she felt sorry for me. I was prepared to reject her pity, but her eyes let me know that she understood there was something deeper going on with me that needed to be rooted out at that very moment, or perhaps I wouldn't even make it home alive.

Then it happened. For the first time in my life I admitted to a complete stranger that I was an alcoholic and that I needed help. A flood of shame and unexplainable freedom washed over me as the words spilled out of my mouth. I was ashamed of my current state, and ashamed of becoming the man that I so loathed as a little boy. And yet there was a liberating feeling that warmed me as I confessed my sickness to this woman.

I was crying out for help and a feeling of hope soon enveloped me, a feeling that I hadn't felt for a very long time. Knowing what I know now, this lady had to have been an angel sent by God to save my life.

She took me into a back office of the church and told me that if I decided to choose it, I could have a better life. That I could break free from this disease and live a happy, healthy life. She explained to me that she had been an alcoholic and a drug addict for ten years and got clean. She had been sober for five years and said she had never been happier in her life. She gave me hope that maybe I could live without alcohol, and that one day I could be just like her.

She gave me all the information I needed to get help; names and numbers of rehab centers, halfway houses and local Alcoholic Anonymous meetings. I will never forget that lady as long as I live. God moved through her and saved my life.

Still drinking on the ride home, I wasn't cured just then, but she put the right thoughts in my head and gave me all the information I needed to get help.

I got home and immediately started calling the numbers she had given me. One particular number stuck out to me. It was called The Cat House, an inpatient rehab center.

A couple years back, I was sentenced to an outpatient treatment center through the courts because of a disorderly conduct case. The Cat House was where I had gone. Clearly that rehab center hadn't worked out for me. I would take a six-pack with me in the trunk, and as soon as I left I would crack open my beer on the drive home. I wasn't ready then, and nobody was going to tell me I couldn't drink. I had convinced myself that's what I did and that was who I was.

This time was different. I was at the end of my rope, ready to get help or die trying. I called The Cat House for the next couple of days, leaving messages. And for those couple of days I drank more than ever. I stayed out of my mind and prayed that when I passed out, I wouldn't wake up.

Some say hell is here on earth. Well, I was living in hell for those four days. Voices in my head kept telling me I wasn't nothing without the alcohol and that I should just go ahead and kill myself. Certainly nobody would care or miss me.

I had no strength to fight back. I was powerless to this disease. I was a puppet, and alcohol was my puppet master. All this time I thought I was the man and was in control of everyone and everything around me. It was all just part of the devil's plan to destroy me day by day until he had me right where he wanted me.

On the fourth day of calling The Cat House and leaving messages, I woke up drinking and didn't even know what day it was or how long I had been just sitting in that apartment. I didn't even remember leaving, but I never ran out of beer. I started seeing visions of the devil coming for me and walking me down steep, dark, dirty steps. I could feel the heat. My entire body started to sweat.

Drunk out of my mind, I don't even know how I answered the ringing phone, but it was The Cat House finally returning my call.

"I need help," I told them, and I did. If nothing else, the way I had blown up their phone should have let them know how desperate I was. I was in a dark hole and I was not sure that I would ever get out alive.

"Can you be here first thing in the morning?" was what the person on the other end of the line said to me. "If you can't, we will have to give the spot to someone else."

"I promise I will be there! Please don't give that spot to anyone else. I'm desperate and I can't do this by myself. Please, I need your help!"

I called my baby sister and asked her to take me to The Cat House the next day, to which she agreed to do.

That night seemed like an eternity. I had plenty of beer and drank every can with a sense of urgency. I had a fight with the devil that night. He tried to take my life and almost succeeded.

It's hard for me to put into words the events of that night. It was the worst night of my life. The only way I can think to describe it is mental torture. The devil took me to the lowest point in my human existence. He sat right across the table from me and put me down by using flashbacks of all the horrible things I'd done in my life; the driving with my kids in the car while I was drunk; all the affairs that I had; all the people I put my hands on. The devil showed me all the women crying because I'd hurt their feelings.

I get goose bumps just writing these words that I have never told a soul. I don't know why my life was spared that night. I know that many people in that space have overdosed or committed suicide. For some reason God decided to spare my life to get to the next day.

That night it was just me and the devil sitting at the table like we were watching a movie of my life . . . and it was all bad; not one good scene. He was trying to kill me and I had no more will left in me. I was ready to give up. Then there was a knock at the door. It was Kyle, my sister's husband.

Sometimes when one is drowning, a lifeline is thrown to allow the person to hold on a little longer until they can be saved. My heart told me that my lifeline had just arrived.

Chapter Four

Taking Some Suggestions

I left the apartment headed for recovery. Here I was a forty-four year old, feeling like a scared little eighteen year old boy who was lost and confused about what had become of his life. My addiction had taken everything from me. I was homeless, jobless, and penniless. Very few of my friends or past lovers wanted anything to do with me anymore. All I had to my name walking through those treatment doors was a garbage bag full of clothes. I had no idea what to expect.

I had been through a lot in my life, from landing in jail to putting myself in various life or death situations on a daily basis. But this was one of the most terrifying things that I ever had to do. For the first time in my life, I felt painfully alone and I didn't know what the future had in store for me. This overwhelming uncertainty brought on a uniquely terrifying set of fears.

I got checked in, strip-searched, and then sent to see the doctor for detox medication. I took a drug test and the doctor said that there were all kinds of drugs in my system. The test revealed some drugs that I didn't even remember doing. Then the doctor told me something that sent chills down my spine. He told me that I could die from detoxing off of the alcohol. He gave me the detox medicine and I slept for three days.

The first floor of the rehab center was a series of isolated rooms that resembled jail cells. These rooms were closely monitored, mainly to keep its inhabitants from hurting themselves. First floor patients were kept on this detox level of the center until they had improved enough to move to the second floor, where there was a more liberal level of freedom to move around and interact with other treatment patients. After I detoxed and woke up, they moved me upstairs. I was introduced to my counselor and given a schedule to follow during my stay.

Now that I currently work in a treatment center, I always hear the clients complain about everything. The shape I was in when I got to The Cat House, I was just thankful to have a bed and to be eating three meals a day. I was willing to do anything they told me just so I wouldn't drink again, because I finally had come to fully understand what drinking was doing me.

I met a bunch of nice guys in there. I kept wondering what in the world could have made them become drug addicts. One guy in particular stood out to me. His name was Tony; a tall, medium build, African American gentleman who was hooked on prescription pills. He'd robbed banks to support his habit. He told me that he robbed three banks before he got caught and did eight years in prison, only to get out and relapse as soon as he got home.

I came into treatment feeling like I was the lowest piece of crap on the face of the earth; like the things that I had done I could never come back or recover from. Listening to the other clients' stories showed me that no matter who you are, this disease can attack you and take over your life. I also began to understand that if I took suggestions from those trying to help me, I could recover and stay clean.

I went to every group session while I was in treatment. I made no phone calls home or worried about what was going on in the outside world. I was there for one reason only, and that was to learn about my disease and the things I needed to do to recover.

I had reached the place where I had decided to live and not die. There had to be a reason for my life, and if given a chance, I wanted to find that reason. I wanted to believe that I had a purpose for living and that I had something of value to offer the world. I began to believe that my life had been spared. There just had to be a reason for me not only being given a second chance, but another chance . . . and multiple chances after that.

My counselor was an older gentleman with a full head of silvery grey hair. He was a short guy and very well dressed, down to the shoes that always glistened as if they had just been shined. He had been a counselor for fifteen years and was a recovering addict himself. I could relate to him in many ways. I really learned a great deal from that man that I still apply to my life to this day. And I am thankful for the part he played in my recovery.

At The Cat House, once we were there a while, we were allowed to go to outside meetings. We had to ask someone to take us when they came in for the AA meetings. I had been to court ordered meetings before because of some trouble that I had gotten into, but I never took them seriously. I just went to get my slip signed to satisfy the court and to get them off my back. This time was different. I had an entirely different mindset going into these meetings.

I was excited and scared at the same time. I felt at home knowing that these were people just like me. They understood me because they had been in my shoes. They could teach me how to live without drugs and alcohol.

The key to this recovery thing, I found out, was working the steps, and my sponsor got me right to it. I was told that I had to work on myself in order to change. This was such an easy thing to say, but such an incredibly challenging thing to do. There were moments when I wondered if I really deserved a clean life, or if I had the strength to take advantage of the chance that I had been given to live a life of value.

I put the drugs and alcohol down, now I was left with me, and I had to change my attitude, behaviors, and thinking in order to never drink again. So that's what I did. I came to realize that alcohol was a thief who had come into my life to steal any good thing that I had ever had or desired to have. Alcohol had been introduced as a friend, but had shown itself to be an evil enemy capable of taking my life.

They talked about a spiritual awakening in the program, and that's what the steps were for me. After I completed them, I felt like a new man. Up until that point, alcohol and drugs had ruled my life. I had been a slave to it. But now I was free and could write my own story for the rest of my life.

We hit many walls in the recovery process. One of mine early on was that all my life I worked meaningless jobs, and at forty-four years old, I had no trade or career. I started to get down and depressed, so I tried to get back into school. It was difficult because I had flunked out at eighteen because of my addiction, so I had delinquent school loans. I set up a plan to begin paying off the debt. Once I paid back the loans for eight months, I would then be allowed to return to school.

It was always my dream to be a college graduate, but my addiction had robbed me of that dream. I stayed patient, and within a year I was able to go back to school. Some things in life are worth fighting for. I believe that one's dreams are such a thing. For years I had no expectations of a better future. Once I finally had them, I didn't want to easily let them go.

Chapter Five
Now I'm Here

Once I got enrolled in a local community college, I found that I loved every minute of my college experience and wouldn't trade it for the world. I went to school for substance abuse counseling, considering all I knew was alcohol and drugs. I felt like my experiences could help someone just like that lady in the church had helped me. The program taught me that I have to give it away to keep it. In other words, sharing my story with others would become a key to maintaining my recovery.

I learned that I should embrace my painful background while realizing that it was my pain that allowed me to relate to recovering addicts, just like the gray haired man had so easily related to me. Maybe I hadn't wasted forty-four years of my life. Maybe I was just being prepared to be able to help others.

While I was working on earning my associate's degree, I got a job working as a treatment assistant at a local inpatient rehab center and I loved it. I remember the first time I went there with my sponsor to a meeting. I fell in love with the center and its program. It was at that moment that I said to myself that one day I would be a counselor there. I could see myself helping to lead fellow addicts away from the substances that were so willing to utterly destroy them. I wanted so desperately to do for others what had been done for me.

Because of my passion for helping recovering addicts, I quickly moved through several positions in the organization. I did many different jobs, taking the time to learn everything I could about the counseling process. Meanwhile, while attending community college, I was learning the technical terms, policies, and procedures of addiction counseling.

I graduated from Columbus State Community College with a 3.5 GPA. I got my associate's degree in Social and Human Services. Unlike my high school graduation, I walked across the stage. Holding that degree in my hands was one of the greatest feelings I had ever felt. I did have value! I was worth something and I was now prepared to make a difference!

Upon attaining my Associates Degree in Drug and Addiction Counseling, I was promoted to the position of counselor just like I had dreamed.

Sometimes I sit and wonder, Why me? With all the people locked up in jail for life with drug related crimes, and all the people dying of overdoses and alcohol related deaths, why did I make it out? Why was I blessed to escape my life of alcohol, drugs, and a certain early death?

I fall to my knees every morning and thank God for the chances He has given me, and all the people along the way that helped me stay sober. I couldn't have done it without each and every one of them. I can truly say, "I started from the bottom, now I'm here."

I believe that God has always had a plan for me to help save His people that are lost just like I was. And unlike when I was in my addiction being selfish and self-centered, I have learned that helping others fills that void that I had been missing my entire life.

Every time a client knocks on my office door, I'm reminded of God's plan for me . . . and perhaps the person's on the other side of that door.

Now I'm Here

Part III

"Monsters in the Pews"

(Jill Lundy's Story)

Chapter One
Fear and Courage are Siamese Twins

I'm sitting in the middle of the floor looking at lights on a Christmas tree, amazed at how shiny, bright, and colorful all the lights are. The room itself is dark, but the lights on the tree fill the room with magic and excitement. I must be two or three years old. I live in Youngstown, Ohio. My mom is nearby and my daddy is upstairs. I'm happy.

I have few, but fond, fleeting memories of living in Youngstown, Ohio as a small girl. I remember sneaking sips of coffee with cream and sugar from my dad's white coffee mug. He often came home from work so late that it would almost be time for him to wake up in the morning and go to work again. He would sit in his favorite recliner awaiting breakfast, and then fall asleep.

I had a German Shepherd named King Jerry who lived outside in a dog house. We often went to my Grandmother Lottie's house. She had green grape vines growing off the fence in her backyard. The grapes were always a little sour, but so fun to pick, and so delicious.

I encountered my first bully in Youngstown at about the age of four. A huge girl who was riding a pretty big, two-wheel bicycle told me that she would beat me up if I didn't immediately get on that bike and ride it. That day I learned that fear can be a powerful motivator.

I rode the bike without falling. I was the only four year old riding a bike that big. I think I learned that all fear doesn't necessarily result in negative outcomes. Sometimes you learn incredible things about yourself that can cause you to have the courage to overcome obstacles and beat the odds. So, I guess my earliest recollection of being courageous was at that particular age; at the behest of being scared to death. Yes, fear and courage are Siamese twins. You can't have one without the other.

Chapter Two

Whoever Said the Boogie-Man Isn't Real . . . LIED!

"Daddy, please don't leave. If you leave, a monster will get me!" I stood at the front door crying hysterically and gripped with fear, watching my parents drive away.

My parents were ministers and teachers. There was always a service, an event, or a meeting that required their presence. So in come the babysitters.

As children, my two sisters, brother and I had what seemed to be 1000 uncles, aunties, and cousins, all comprised of friends, family, and close associates of my parents. Many were members of their church who became endeared friends. It was usually from this pool of people that a babysitter was selected. Most of these individuals could be described as some of the most wonderful human beings on the planet. They showed us kindness, humor, and lots of love. Everyone appeared to love my parents in this group, but someone betrayed them. There was a monster, or two, in the midst.

Hide-and-seek time seemed like the monster's favorite game. I was in the middle of the floor, my parents were gone, and the Boogie-man was in my house. I had to quickly find a place to hide. The closet was a no go, but perhaps I could hide under my bed.

Wrong!

The Boogie-man was in my room.

The Boogie-man got me.

Chapter Three
Thieves in the Temple

"Love come QUICK, Love come in a HURRY . . . There are thieves in the temple tonight."

I wasn't sure who Prince was referring to when he wrote those lyrics, but oh, if he only knew.

I had learned that monsters are real, and they lurked all around, even sometimes in my house. But dear God, monsters are allowed to attack inside the church; even inside the very sanctuary?

"No, of course not," you say. Then explain this:

I was coming out of a youth choir rehearsal when everyone else had gone outside. I had to go to the bathroom, so I stayed behind. As I came back out of the bathroom, I quickly recognized that the lights had been turned off in the church.

I determined that I needed to get out of there with quickness. The most direct way to get to the front of that particular church was by going back out through the main sanctuary. Easy enough, I figured, so I entered the sanctuary and began walking from the altar area to the back entrance doors. It was a fairly large space, so quickly and alone, I walked through the darkness. Then I heard a sound.

It was footsteps.

I wasn't alone after all.

I couldn't see anyone because it was so dark. My heart skipped a beat. I stopped dead in my tracks and looked around, trying to hear whoever it was that was in the sanctuary with me. All I could hear was movement. Someone was getting closer to me, but they were not saying anything.

I'm scared!

I ducked down and began to crawl between the pews in the sanctuary, trying to get to the back door, but more importantly, trying not to be heard.

I heard someone close to the pew where I was crawling. I got completely under it so that I was unable to be seen between the pews. Before I knew it, someone jumped in front of my pew. Now I was terrified.

A large hand grabbed my ankle. I screamed and tried to scurry away. It was a man. I could tell by his big, rough hands. I could smell him.

He pulled me from under the pew and back toward him. He then jumped on top of me. I was flailing my arms and trying to push him away.

I know who this is. I could clearly recognize him now. He was the pastor's grandson! He wasn't a man. He was a boy. He was actually my age; a teenager, but he was much bigger than me. He had to have been at least six feet and three inches tall, while I was only about five feet and three inches tall. He was HUGE to me, and pretty strong. History had already taught me that in that type of circumstance to FIGHT . . . somehow.

"What are you doing?" I asked him while trembling. "Get off me! Get off!"

He didn't say anything. He just grabbed my arms and pinned me to the floor . . . in the sanctuary.

"Stop! Get off me!" I continued to yell.

He hit me in my mouth and told me to shut up. He tried to kiss me in the mouth, I think. I turned my head and he licked my face.

I continued to struggle. He pulled open my blouse while trying to secure his body on top of me and between my legs. I kept fighting, and then he hit me in my stomach, slightly knocking the wind out of me.

"Be still," he told me.

"No. Just Stop. Let me go!"

He hit me again and was able to force his body between my legs. He laid his upper body on top of my face and put his hands down my panties. Suddenly, the front door of the sanctuary opened.

We both heard it.

He immediately froze. After a couple seconds he got up and ran away, leaving me shaking and scared to death.

"Hey, who's in here?"

I recognized that voice. It was my attacker's father.

I panicked because I didn't know how to explain what had just happened. How was I supposed to tell him that it was his son who had just fled the scene?

Words escaped me, so I joined them in an escape.

I chose to run. I didn't know what else to do.

I ran out of the sanctuary and downstairs into a women's lounge. I got into a closet and hid. Shaking, crying, and feeling sick, I hid.

Within minutes, the father was coming down the stairs that led into the lounge. He demanded that I come out.

"I know someone is in here, so come on out," he said.

I was so scared. I didn't want to give up my hiding place, but he started yelling at me, insisting that I come out. So I did.

As soon as he saw me, he noticed that my shirt was open. "Who was in there with you?" were the words he spoke.

I didn't answer, and so he asked again, a bit more loudly and with more authority.

"Your son," my nervous lips spoke.

He stared at me momentarily before saying, "Clean yourself up and get outside." He immediately left the lounge, but not before looking at me with disdain.

I was confused. Clean myself up? What the heck did that mean? Wasn't he going to go after his son and get to the bottom of things?

I went into the bathroom, washed my face, pulled my clothes together, and then went outside. I thought the worst of the trouble was over, but oh was I wrong. I had now been marked. Trouble had just announced its arrival to my world, and it decided to attach itself to me.

"No Safety Under the Pews"

Chapter Four

The Smear Campaign ... Adding Insult to Injury

I became the girl with the scarlet letter. There was a deliberate effort to "protect" a son who committed an evil deed. Instead of insisting that my attacker take responsibility for his evil deed, I was made an instant villain by a few of the adults in the church family. I was ostracized, isolated, and very quickly became "persona non grata" within our youth group and the youth choir.

I felt like I was being treated like I had the plague. I was given the reputation of being a siren, a succubus, a slut. Any encounter I had involving a male was automatically seen as me being "fast." In truth, at times I probably was being fast. However, during that stage of life, I was naturally curious about the physical changes occurring with my body. I also became interested in experimentation with intimate encounters. Not to mention the desire to be a normal youth and gain acceptance from my peers by attempting to participate in all the same activities that everyone was participating in at the time. In the end, the outcome always seemed a little different for me.

Anyone who chose to interact with me was given the evil eye. I was cornered and interrogated in the bathroom. "What is going on with you and that boy you're always hanging around with?"

I attempted to disclose to one of the adults supervising the youth that something "sexually inappropriate" had happened to me.

The response I heard from another adult in leadership who was within earshot was, "I wouldn't touch that with a ten foot pole."

I strongly felt that there was a specific effort to even turn my own sisters against me. My brother never participated in the church madness at all, but I believe my sisters were manipulated and convinced that they, too, should denounce me because I was the "trouble maker."

I'm not sure if any other family members of my attacker, or any other youth choir members, actually knew what happened during that encounter—outside of rumor—but I do know that although I was permitted to remain in the group, I was actually all alone.

Much to my dismay, there happened to be members of my attacker's family who were very influential in the communities at large. They had many local and distant connections. Some so distant that I was once confronted at my school about the "sanctuary scandal." My school was in a different city altogether, so I was surprised that the news had even traveled there to haunt me.

"I heard about the things that happened with you at your church. My mom said that you got kicked out of your church because you was always in trouble, and the last straw was that you got caught having sex with the pastor's son inside the church."

This bathroom gossip was filled with inaccurate information; a total disregard to the truth. But then again, gossipers always distort facts.

The truth of the matter was that eventually my parents left that church to go to another one in a different city, taking me and my sisters with them. Although I don't recall ever disclosing the details of what happened that night in the sanctuary with my parents, they became quite aware that I was receiving some unfair treatment. I'm not sure what type of backlash came to them, if any at all, but I always felt that the ultimate reason we left that church somehow centered on me.

Unfortunately, I honestly believed that my sisters also felt that we'd left that church because of me. In my mind, that added fuel to an already blazing fire. My perception was that my sisters became very angry with me and blamed me for causing them to have to leave all their friends and break the relationships that they had established. In hindsight, I believe they were manipulated and put in a position where they had to choose me, the "trouble maker," or the powers that be at the church. That affected their ability to be a part of the youth group and have access to their friends.

While that may not be accurate at all in reality, the way I saw it, my sisters chose the church group and their friends over me. That was my perception at the time, and a very painful reality for me.

My parents chose to move on nonetheless. They always seemed to feel they had spiritual assignments at various churches, and I would probably agree that that was true. But that time I felt that the underlying reason for the move was me. It was at that point that things became extremely tense at home between me and my sisters. I know they loved me, but I think my situation was the cause of a huge rift between us. I'm positive to this day that they probably had no idea of what was truly going on.

Either way, I was once again feeling alienated and alone. I didn't have the means to escape what I thought was venom being directed toward me by my sisters over the loss of their friends. Eventually, I began to retaliate. I became very confrontational at home, and I became extremely good at arguing, releasing anger, resentment, and venom of my own.

If I could go back and change anything, it would be to have somehow protected myself and my sisters from the divisive attack that was mounting against us and changed how we interacted with each other for quite some time.

There was always much love, but there was also constant tension. Much of the tension, no doubt, was initiated by me, because at the end of the day, I felt betrayed and like I was less important than my sister's friends.

In short, I felt inferior.

Chapter Five

No Rest for the Weary

My life at home was sour and things at school were crazy. Rumors continued to mount and tensions with my classmates and others in my church world continued to be a source of frustration and anxiety. It didn't matter whether people knew me or not. Everyone in my world seemed to be able to see the scarlet letter stamped on my chest. I was pressured daily at school to have sexual contact with boys; some who pretended that they actually liked me and wanted to be my friend. Sometimes I'd get cornered while at school, but I would primarily get harassed outside while simply walking through my neighborhood.

There were three boys from my school who constantly harassed and badgered me. The harassment was usually centered on forcefully touching my breasts and genitalia, and the boys insisting and pressuring me to touch them.

I became convinced that there must have actually been something wrong with me. "I must really be a slut," I would tell myself. I had been called the derogatory term so many times, and I must have deserved all the treatment that I was getting. I had to have been bringing it upon myself. I started to believe that everything that was said about me must have been true. So I would reluctantly go along with their sexual bullying until I could get away from these boys.

One day after school, this particular trio of boys decided to follow me home; taunting me and teasing me until I got fairly close to my house. I was nervous because I was by myself and outnumbered by them. One of them was actually the boyfriend of my only and best friend. I tried to get a sense of what their intentions were, but I had an idea that it was not good at all. The mean and malicious things that they were saying to me assured me that there wasn't anything good coming out of the situation. I just wanted to get home.

Finally I got close to my house. They were neighbors, so they also lived in close proximity to me. One actually lived directly across the street from me. This is important to note, because I guess they had been watching me for a while. As I got closer to my house, I noticed that there was no car in the driveway. I knew that meant no one was home, and the boys came to the same conclusion.

When I realized these guys weren't leaving me alone, I quickly made a dash toward my house by picking up my pace. They actually began to pick up their pace too. I had nowhere to run or hide outside, so I ran into my house and shut the door where I thought I was safe.

I heard the boys talking outside my door, but I couldn't quite make out what they were saying. They knocked on my door. I didn't answer. No one answered. That was their confirmation that I was, in fact, home alone. I thought surely they would just leave, but I began to understand that these boys were actually predators, and it seemed like I was the prey.

I hadn't locked the door when I ran inside my house. I originally didn't think it would matter, but I was still uncomfortable, so I went toward the door to lock it. As I started going toward the door from another room, I heard the boys actually right outside the door. I could hear that they were in the process of opening it.

Shocked and in disbelief, I grabbed a knife from the kitchen and immediately ran downstairs into my mother's study. I hid in the closet. These boys didn't know the layout of my house, so they were not aware of all the spaces in the house. But I could hear their footsteps. They were in my home!

As I remained hidden, I could hear them talking.

"She couldn't have gotten out of the house," one said. "We were all right here."

"Yeah," another agreed. "So she has to be in here."

They began to search and taunt. "We know you're in here."

"You know we're going to find you."

How in the world were they so bold, and how were they so sure that no one would come home?

Search if they might, they couldn't find me. After about ten minutes, their voices were distant, and then I heard my house door open and close. I thought they must have gone, but I didn't trust my instinct, so I stayed in the closet.

Although my house remained quiet, I just sat there with the knife in hand. I was frazzled and didn't know exactly what would happen next. After a few more minutes, the house phone rang. I got hopeful. I knew at that point I could at least talk to someone; perhaps even get someone to come to my house.

I came out of the closet to answer the phone, and there they were . . . two of them, just waiting for me. I ran and grabbed the phone and answered it. It was my best friend's boyfriend at the house across the street from me. It was a trap. They had set me up to get me out of the closet. Their intentions were now obvious. My best friend's boyfriend returned to my house where I was then gang raped at knife point by all three boys. In the initial struggle of the boys trying to get the knife away from me, I got cut on my leg. I still have the scar. Both the physical one and mental one.

Chapter Six

And Rapists Remain Free

This must have been my fault, I thought. How could I have let them get into my house? After the sexual assault, I called my best friend from my old neighborhood, as we had recently moved into the current neighborhood just about a year or two prior to this incident. I called her crying hysterically, probably in shock, and I told her what happened. I told her I was bleeding on my leg because I had been cut.

"You have to call the police!"

"No one will believe me because they were inside my house. How can I explain that?"

She didn't know, but she didn't care. "You have to call the police. Call them now!"

I, on the other hand, was dealing with what I knew about my current situation. I was the SLUT. I'd been here before where I had told the truth, and I ended up being the one to blame. So, I decided to say nothing.

I was tortured every day when I went to school. Because I had to see those boys, I was fearful that something awful was going to happen. Approximately three months went by, and something awful happened indeed. I suddenly began to get very sick. My mother finally took me to the doctor's office. I was fourteen years old. I was also pregnant. What would I do now? How could I explain being pregnant?

My mother didn't look at me with disgust or disappointment in her eyes; she looked at me with love, compassion, confusion, and concern. I was just flat numb. I didn't know what to say, not even when she asked me who the father was.

I busted out in tears upon her inquiry. "Mommy, I don't know." At that point, I began to disclose and tell her the whole terrible truth about being raped in my own home.

When we got back home after leaving the doctor's office, the first thing my mom did was tell my dad. Once my brother found out he was furious. My parents had to keep him from going after the boys. So instead of my brother taking the law into his own hands, my parents called the police.

A police report was filed. I'm assuming the boys were arrested; all but one of them that is. My best friend's boyfriend. I conveniently left his name out of the report, although he was the one who sprang the trap. He was also, however, my only friend's boyfriend. I didn't want her to know what he had done. I concluded she would be devastated, and wasn't sure what would happen to our friendship.

Because of this error in judgement on my part, when he came forward on behalf of the other boys, he told the police that he, in fact, had been at my house, and that they all "had sex" with me. So, with that and the facts that too much time had passed and, I didn't inform the police of the incident when it originally occurred, and the parents of my friend who I called immediately after would not allow her to get involved and make a statement on my behalf, the case was dropped.

I was sent to a psychologist. While she believed my story, she also concluded that given the circumstances, it was her professional opinion that I should have an abortion, as the "psychological burden" of having the child would be too much for someone so young to bear.

I didn't understand the total implication of what she'd said.

"You need to consider carefully what the psychologist said and make a decision to the best of your ability," my mother told me. "I will support whatever decision you make."

My mother's words were comforting. My father, on the other hand, had very strong convictions regarding the entire situation.

I believe he was in conflict with himself. He was conflicted with what he was taught to believe from his Christian theology. The psychologist was relentless and was pretty adamant about the course of action I should take. I actually didn't want to have an abortion, but I was scared about everything. The one and only thing that stuck with me were words I heard my father saying to my mother and the psychologist.

"This is too much. I just hate this. How could this happen to my baby girl?"

I'd never heard my father say that he hated anything. I was so sad and full of conflict myself. I didn't know what to do.

With all of that burned into my brain, I complied with the wishes of the psychologist, and with a broken heart, I went like a lamb to the slaughter and had an abortion. It was like being raped a thousand times over. Although I cried during the procedure, I never said a word.

It was DONE! With that act, it was confirmed for me that at 14 years of age, not only was I truly a slut, but I was now also a murderer. At least that's what they'd taught me in the church I was so diligently attending. So then there was the question that rested on my mind and in my heart: Does God forgive murderers?

Chapter Seven

Ooh-oo Child, Things are Gonna get Easier . . . NOT Yet

Every morning that I woke up I felt nervous and sick to my stomach. What would await me when I had to go back to school? That question plagued my mind. Then the day finally came when I had to face my fears and return to school after not having attended since reporting the boys to the police.

What was going to happen today? Nervousness started from the moment I got to the bus stop. When we expect bad things to happen, we may occasionally be granted our expectations. On that particular day my fears were realized. As sure as the sun came up in the morning, the twins, "Drama" and "Trauma," greeted me in my very first class. It was a Monday, a couple of weeks after the abortion.

In all of my classes I always sat in the middle of the front row or as close to that as possible. That way I only had my teachers and their notes in my view. It gave me an excuse to attempt to become invisible. I was taking notes. I had no time to engage in conversation or clown around with classmates. However, that particular classroom's set-up was a little different from some of the others. The entrance was at the front instead of the back, so I had to see everyone who came in the classroom after me.

As I sat waiting for the start of class, the tardy bell rang. The teacher began to start his lesson when one of my attackers entered the room. The teacher asked him if he had a pass because he was late.

Instead of answering the teacher, he looked directly at me and then charged toward me, attacking me while I was sitting in my seat.

It was one of those desk with the chair attached, so I could not get out of the seat. When he jumped on me, the chair flew back with me in it. He began hitting me and I hit the floor. Very quickly, the teacher, and I think another student, grabbed him, allowing me to get out of the seat. Someone whisked me out of the room and to the nurse's office. It turned out that my right thumb was broken. I was absolutely horrified. The boy was suspended from school, but the assault was labeled "a fight," which meant he could return to school after only a few days of suspension.

Things became increasingly challenging at home and at school. I had friends at the church we were currently attending, but I was so sad and so scared all of the time. I felt like I was suffocating. It was the first time that I began to think about dying. I just wanted to stop being scared. To stop being so sad. To stop the constant noise in my head that caused me to be in so much pain. I just wanted it all to STOP!

Instead of trying to kill myself at that time, I ran away from home. I ran to the city that I lived in just prior to moving to my current residence. It was a place I was familiar with, and a place where I felt I had a friend or two. It really didn't matter; it was a place that was just . . . away.

When I arrived to the area, it was already dark outside. I wasn't very prepared. After all, I had never run away from home before. I had no food, no money, not even a jacket. The weather was pretty warm during the day, but I didn't realize that it would actually get so cold at night. So there I was in the city, cold with no place to go.

I found myself at the junior high school that I last attended when I lived there. There were lights near the entranceway doors, and at the doors there was also a cove-like space that provided a little shelter from the wind. My first night out, I huddled down on the ground in the space in front of a door at the school, and that is where I stayed that night. I tried to get some sleep, but I heard dogs and critters, and it was cold. Needless to say, sleep was hard to come by.

The next morning, I found myself at the house of a friend from seventh grade. He realized that I had run away and he tried to help. During the day he allowed me to hang out in his garage. We talked about so many things. When night fell, he snuck me into the basement inside his house and allowed me to sleep in a space that was dug out between the foundation of the house and the cement wall in the basement. It was his little hiding space.

The next morning after my first night there, he disclosed to me all the troubles that he was having in his life. He offered me my first taste of alcohol. It was vodka . . . straight. He shared with me the fact that at the young age of fourteen, he was already an alcoholic.

"I know that things are rough for you right now," he told me, "but you don't want to end up like me. You have a mom and dad that are probably worried out of their minds about you right now."

He basically gave me the "come to Jesus" speech that suggested I get over myself and go home.

It had been almost two days since I'd run away from home when he told me, "I'm not going to be able to hide you much longer. You're going to have to go home."

I wasn't ready to go home, but I had to leave, so I left his home and went back to the housing development that I lived in when we resided in that area. I ran into a friend and came up with some story that caused her mom to allow me to spend the night, but I had to leave that next morning.

So morning came and I left. At that point I had been gone for four days and three nights. A former neighbor saw me hanging around, spoke to me, and recognized that I was in the neighborhood alone. She invited me to come to her house. After questioning me about what I was doing in the area alone, she became suspicious. Being a responsible and caring adult, she called my parents and put me on the phone with them.

I spoke to my mother and she asked me if I was ready to come home. After answering in the negative, she then asked me if I would come home. I found her second query interesting. It was almost like I honestly had a choice. For once in my life someone was giving me a choice without pressure.

Before I answered, she suggested that I meet with her and my dad at a restaurant in the area so that we could talk. I agreed to do so.

When I arrived at the restaurant, my parents were already there. I went to their table and my dad stood up and hugged me. He was crying. Sobbing, he told me he thought he'd never see me again. He said he believed he was going to get a call from someone saying that they found me, but that I was dead. That was an unbearable thought for him. I later found out that he'd cried straight for the entire three days I was gone. I returned home that day with my parents.

Once back at home, things were increasingly tense between my sisters and me. My brother never really got involved in any of the craziness and was no longer living at home. By that time he had joined the US Navy and was living in Scotland. My parents were very happy that I was home and tried to provide encouragement and support the best that they could. It was just a difficult time.

Chapter Eight
Still I Rise

As a result of all that had recently transpired, my parents removed me from the school that I had been attending. They enrolled me into a private Christian school located on the other side of town. I had to be bussed, so it took an hour to get to school. It was probably the best thing that could have happened to me at the time. I could finally begin to breathe and feel safe at school, as my experience at this school was immediately different, and much more positive.

It wasn't long before I got involved in sports and began cheerleading for the basketball team during the winter. In the spring I ran track and became a sprinter.

As far as my academics were concerned, I began to excel. I was getting really good grades and I very quickly achieved honor roll status. Ultimately, by the end of the first and second semester, I was a Dean's List honoree. It was at that time I began to realize that there *was* actually something good about me. I was athletic and SMART!

With a newly found internal inspiration, I purposed in my heart and mind that I would go to college and "BE SOMEBODY!"

At the end of my sophomore year in high school, my family moved to the West Coast. I was enrolled in school as a high school junior, and once again I was the new kid on the block.

The schools in the West Coast were quite different than those in the Midwest and East Coast. What stood out most was the size of the schools. They were huge! It was average for a school to have 3,000 plus students. They had outdoor campus style schoolyards containing several buildings instead of just one school building like I'd been used to attending. I'd never been exposed to an environment like that one. So, as it were, my junior year of high school was without any major incident. I basically got lost in the shuffle.

I didn't really have any friends. It was extremely difficult for me to penetrate the cliques there. Needless to say, it was a very lonely year. I had my studies and I continued to strive for academic excellence.

By my senior year in high school, I not only maintained my previous honor roll status, but I had also been accepted into a program for students who desired to have a career in the medical field. It was the perfect opportunity for a "Daddy's Girl" whose father was also a medical doctor. So, in my senior year, I was bussed more than an hour away to the Medical Magnet School.

The school was located in Southern California and affiliated with USC Medical Center. While attending the magnet school, I had the opportunity to do an internship where I worked in a medical research lab. I participated in a study that was looking at the effects of radiation on bovine serum albumin. Bovine serum albumin is a serum albumin protein derived from cows. It is often used as a protein concentration standard in lab experiments.

My senior year was not a huge social success; being the new outsider again. It was however, extremely exciting because it opened me up to new ideas, hopes, and dreams. I graduated from high school as an honor student. It was now time to seriously consider my future. I decided that I definitely wanted to follow in my dad's footsteps and become a medical professional. I knew the road for that would be long and bumpy, but I was up for the challenge. After all, my entire life had been a challenge . . . so still I rise!

Chapter Nine

I'm a Survivor

The time came when I decided to thrust myself into the world of young adulthood as a college freshman at the largest university in the United States at that time, which happened to be three thousand miles away from my parents. I chose to attend The Ohio State University in Columbus, Ohio.

It was the boldest step I'd made in my life since running away from home. The reality of this venture was extremely exciting and overwhelming at the same time. I believe the only reason I was able to get to my dorm and feel like I would be able to manage was because of the guardian angel waiting for me when I arrived in Columbus, Ohio.

I had a "Big Brother" there. My God Brother to be exact.

It was he who greeted me once I arrived in Ohio, escorted me to the university, and basically moved me into Taylor Tower, the "Honors Dorm."

I think what was most impactful about the interaction was a particular incident that gave me courage and confidence to go forward. There were three small but powerful statements that my brother spoke to me before he left.

He reached over, hugged me and said, "I love you, and I'm really proud of you. You're going to do well." Eventually, that is exactly what happened. But it was not without some epic failures first.

It was extremely exciting for me to live on campus. I absolutely loved it. However, there was immense pressure associated with being at a university so far out of my comfort zone, and away from my major support system; my parents. The culture and environment at the university was unlike anything I had ever experienced. Many people that I attached myself to at that time had both positive and negative effects on me. I affiliated myself with some of the more "colorful individuals" on campus, and my life was beginning to move very fast.

I never got involved with drugs and alcohol. I had one roommate that I befriended who did drink. We took up with a few associates on campus who indulged in both alcohol and drugs. They seemed to party all the time. On some occasions my roommate and I stayed out with them very late into the night.

I was totally immersed in my new lifestyle of hanging out, staying up all night, and even occasionally "hooking up" sexually with a guy here and there. I was lost, and I didn't realize the negative toll that it was taking on me. My grades began to suffer for the first time in several years. I lost my focus and began to drown in the whirlpool that had I put myself into. Ultimately, because I was in a downward spiral with grades and associations, that old familiar feeling of depression and fear began to eat away at me. I was afraid I was becoming a disappointment. I was afraid that I was becoming a failure.

By the fourth quarter of my freshman year, I had become affiliated with a psychology support group on campus through one of my psych classes. By then I had also met and started dating a guy that

I was absolutely crazy about. He called himself "Kenny Wayne Easy-Ellison." Kenny E. for short.

I spent lots of time with Kenny; as much as I could as a matter of fact. He was like a breath of fresh air. When we were together, we laughed, cuddled, and always talked about our dreams and the future. But when he was away, I was consumed with thoughts of failure, death, and dying.

I once opened up to Kenny about how I was feeling. He was shocked. He never saw my emotional whirlwind coming, but he spent time talking to me about what I was going through. He ultimately convinced me that my thinking was scary and dangerous. He insisted that I share what was going on with me in my support group, so I did. The outcome of that decision created an unintended turn of events that basically resulted in me being involuntarily admitted into the University Hospital's Young Adult Psychiatric Unit, diagnosed with Suicidal Ideation, Depression, and Bulimia; an eating disorder.

I think deep on the inside, I was pretty upset with Kenny because I got locked down; but I presume that he was even more upset with me. I clearly hadn't disclosed to him how serious my feelings and behaviors were. Although we were close, he had absolutely no idea that I was indeed bulimic or suicidal.

As the can of worms of disclosure opened, Kenny discovered that I had once previously "hooked up" with a good friend of his brother's, whom Kenny was also well acquainted with. I just failed to mention that small detail to him. Nonetheless, he felt deceived, and possibly even betrayed. Even still, he looked beyond it and insisted that the more important issue at hand was to take care of what was obviously on the verge of killing me.

He helped me conclude that it was best at that time for me to return home to California where I could be under the care and supervision of my parents. Leaving him was one of the most difficult and heart wrenching things that I had to do. But it was necessary. I cried throughout the entire flight back to California, as I felt I was losing a part of myself; the good part.

Once I left Columbus, I quickly lost contact with Kenny. I credit him with being the one who, at that juncture, literally saved my life. It would be nearly twenty-eight years later before I got in contact with Kenny again. When I did connect with him, I was simply overwhelmed with joy. I was finally able to thank him for caring for me enough to look past his frustration and disappointment, and tend to my immediate need. He helped me face my demons of fear and depression. He gave me the desire to fight for my life. To this day, I consider Kenny Wayne Easy-Ellison to be one of the most influential people in my life, and one of my absolute heroes.

Chapter Ten
And So Life Goes On

Once I was back in California with my family, I decided to go to a trade school to be a medical assistant. My father had always insisted that we acquire marketable skills so that we could survive in the world. I became a Certified Medical Assistant within nine months. I was hired to work in an office that specialized in industrial medicine; which was basically industrial injuries on the job. Needless to say, that was a pretty traumatizing introduction into the medical field. It was so traumatic that I decided to return back to The Ohio State University two years later, where my major had been changed from pre-medicine to a major in psychology.

During the next four and a half years, I was quite focused and driven. As a result, I was recognized as a stellar student. I had the privilege to become a Resident Advisor and President of the Delta Phi Chapter of Sigma Gamma Rho Sorority, Inc., which was located on campus. I worked diligently with the Department of Residence and dining halls during the summers as a student counselor during summer orientation and a Service and Support staff member during summer conference housing.

By the time it was all said and done, I received various certificates and awards, including the President's "Excellent Student" Citation. During my final quarter before graduation, I was selected to represent the university as an international student in the Study Abroad Program in Spain.

I graduated from The Ohio State University with a major in Psychology and a minor in Spanish. It would seem that my life had come together and that I would be on my way to making it in the world as a productive member of society. However, I failed to mention that although I had become a stellar student, I never discontinued engaging in relationships with males on campus. It was out of one of these relationships that, not long after graduating from the university, I became a wife and a mother. It was a turbulent and disappointing relationship that soon ended in divorce, resulting in my becoming a single mother.

It was my degree in psychology that would dictate the direction I would pursue in my efforts to become gainfully employed. I became a licensed social worker and had the opportunity to work in various capacities, but primarily with youth agencies. I worked in a residential youth treatment facility for youth ages 10-18 years of age. I also worked as a social worker in treatment foster care. I ultimately ended up working for the Ohio Department of Youth Services as a social worker inside the correctional facilities.

Work was stressful but steady. However, in my personal life, I was thrust into a whirlwind of drama and trauma where I seemed to be cast aimlessly through time and space. There didn't seem to be any apparent rhyme or reason for the events that were taking place in my life . . . until 9/11. After 9/11 I had an epiphany. Prior to that unforgettable day where the Twin Towers fell to the ground as a result of terrorism, I had been somewhat detached from my immediate family. After that day, though, family became an immediate and important focus for me.

Interestingly, as life would have it, I was confronted with a situation involving one of my siblings and her children. In an effort to be most supportive to my sibling, I packed up my world—children included—left the Ohio Department of Youth Services, and I also left the man that I was in a very serious relationship with. I did all of that and moved to Baltimore, Maryland to be with my sister. It seemed like the right thing to do because I could be a help to a dear family member.

I worked within one state system, so I should have easily been able to transfer into another state position in Maryland. That was my thought process anyway. However, it was not the reality once I arrived in Baltimore. I was now in a new state, unemployed, and unable to be hired with the State of Maryland. It was an incredibly serious and frightening circumstance.

It was out of that circumstance that I called upon and utilized one of my "marketable skills," which just so happened to be in the fitness industry. I became a full-time fitness professional. As a result of making such a spontaneous career change, the unimaginable happened. Somehow, by being immersed in the world of fitness, I developed a very strong desire to become competitive in the fitness industry. I soon found, and fell in love with, competitive bodybuilding. I could have never foreseen that I could possibly become a competitive female bodybuilder. But here I am; an International Level Competitive Female Bodybuilding Champion.

Chapter Eleven

Dirt and Pressure Yield Flowers in Full Bloom

"Through many dangers, toils, and snares, I have already come . . ." I see this line from the song "Amazing Grace," written by John Newton, as such an understatement as it relates to my life. There is so much that has transpired in my world; tragedy, failure, and triumph. I recognize that I have successfully managed to achieve a multiplicity of diverse accomplishments throughout my life. I also believe that I still have dreams and goals to fulfill. But where was God in the midst of all that happened in my life? Had God been there every step of my life's journey, directing and orchestrating the outcome? Was there a process that had been preordained by God that I had been going through all this time? What was the point of all I went through in my life? What does it have to do with my ultimate purpose for being on the planet? These are the many questions that constantly plague my mind.

I think the answers to my questions are revealed in the scripture Jeremiah 29:11, which reads:

"For I know the plans I have for you, declares the LORD, plans to prosper you and not to harm you, plans to give you hope and a future."

If I hold that scripture as true, I must concede that there has been purpose to my life from the beginning, and God has been working a plan throughout my life to fulfill that purpose. If I honestly consider the challenges of my early beginnings as well as the challenges I currently face, I must acknowledge that I believe that there has been significant divine intervention that has made it possible for me to accomplish all that I have accomplished. It is because of His plans to cause me no harm but give me hope that has enabled me to stay alive. Because of His plans to give me a future, I am yet compelled, motivated, and inspired to seek an accomplished and full life.

How can I be confident that no matter how devastating and dark the circumstances may have been, God has had plans of hope and a future for me from the beginning? How can I stand in confidence that those plans will be actualized? Well, let's look to nature for an answer. I'll take a practice from the world of horticulture and apply what I have come to know as the "Principle of the Seed."

In this instance, I take rose seeds, I dig a hole, I drop the seed in the hole, I mix in water, and I put a little dirt on top of it. Then I allow that environment to impact, and even nurture the seed. Eventually, I'll watch it grow right out from the depths of the darkness of the hole it was in. As it sheds the dirt that was on top, I can finally witness it materialize into the magnificent flower it was genetically coded to be from the beginning; hope facilitated, surviving the pressure of the environment over time. After withstanding the pressure, the seed now has a future; that is to bloom into a beautiful rose.

Using this analogy, I am the seed. My experiences and circumstances represent being put into the ground in darkness. My failures, depression, and resulting tears represent the water mixed in. Ultimately, my fears and my attempts to conceal and cover up my mess is the dirt on top. In the end, however, that environment, that pressure, the water, and even the darkness nurtured me. It gave me strength to push up out of the hole and shake off the dirt. I emerged as the beautiful prize flower that I was genetically coded from the beginning to be. The actualization of "Super J,'" the Champion Female Bodybuilder is the result!

"And Still I Rise"

That was a clear illustration of how God works His plan throughout every situation for the entire duration of one's life. The process demands that in order to get fruit or a flower, you must have first buried it in a watery pit of darkness covered with dirt, and then waited for the process to allow the potential to unfold. It's all necessary to yield hope and a future, which is God's ultimate plan.

Part IV

"Define Yourself"

(Reuel Barksdale's Story)

Chapter One
There's No Place Like Home

I was born on October 18, 1955. My father was a factory worker and my mother was a homemaker. My mother had two sons from a previous marriage who were grown enough to be out of the house by the time of my birth. My mother and father had a daughter together who was two years older than me. My mother, father, sister, grandmother and I lived in a one floor, 875 square foot home on the west side of Columbus, Ohio.

There were three bedrooms, one bathroom, a living room, kitchen, and utility room where the washer and dryer took up most of the space. My father had purchased our home with a VA loan made possible because of his military service. My neighborhood was full of these track homes. The residents of my neighborhood were blue-collar workers who kept their yards neat and seemed to get along with each other. We had a big backyard and a gravel driveway, which provided parking for my dad's powder blue 1962 Plymouth Valiant.

My Childhood Home

"Mommy, I want fried chicken, candied yams, potato salad, macaroni and cheese, homemade rolls with cherries in the center and glazed tops, yellow cake with chocolate icing, butter pecan ice cream, and sweet tea."

My birthday was always my favorite day of the year. I was permitted to have whatever I wanted for my birthday dinner, and I took full advantage of my freedom to choose. My choices never included vegetables, and for that one day my choices were always granted. I don't remember any of the birthday gifts I may have received, but I will always remember those dinners. I also remember sitting at the kitchen table as my mom sang and made our daily meals.

My mother was the nicest woman I had ever met. I'm sure that like other mere humans, she must have had character flaws, but I honestly cannot identify them. My mother was the epitome of the "sweetly saved" church woman. She didn't smoke, drink, curse, or speak evil about anyone. My mother could sing and had been the director of her choir back in Philadelphia. She cooked breakfast and dinner every day of my childhood.

"Dear God, we thank you for waking us up in our right mind with a desire to serve you. I pray that you give him favor in the sight of men. Keep him from all hurt, harm, and danger."

I would often wake to the sound of my mother praying that very prayer over me. It seemed that she was often praying for my safety and that I would find "favor" in the sight of men.

My father was a no nonsense kind of guy. He stood five feet and ten inches tall, and weighed around two-hundred and forty pounds of mostly muscle. His forearms looked as if he had cable running under his skin. While I never saw my father exercise, he was always walking somewhere or doing some type of manual labor around the house. Walking long distances seemed to be my father's favorite activity. He would often beckon me to join him with little or no warning.

"Come on, Rudy, let's go," my dad would say, calling me by my nickname.

"Yes, sir," I'd reply. "Where are we going?"

"Just for a little walk."

My little, skinny legs had better keep up with him, because he certainly wasn't going to slow down for me. One time we walked from our house to my great grandparents' house on the east side of town.

That had to be at least twenty miles. I never really developed his enthusiasm for walking.

Dad fashioned himself to be a carpenter and a painter with reasonably good skills. He used these skills whenever possible to pick up extra income.

Things were either right or wrong in my father's eyes. There was no in between. He was an orthodox Pentecostal minister who had moved to Columbus, Ohio to attend Aenon Bible College. That is where he and my mom met. My father was an ardent student of the Bible who took every word literally. To my father, doing otherwise would have been a sure ticket to eternal damnation in a fiery hell.

When he wasn't working on something in the house, we could find him reading the scriptures in his chair. My dad definitely believed in the scripture that suggested that sparing the rod would spoil the child. He was determined that his only son would not be spoiled. If he felt his words were not being clearly understood, he was willing and able to let his thick leather belt clarify his thoughts. Needless to say, I was afraid of this man.

Chapter Two

It Takes a Village

The African proverb, "It takes a village to raise a child," has certainly proved to be an altruism in my life. From the age of four and throughout my adolescent years, the village of my childhood provided many memorable lessons. These lessons happened both inside and outside of my home.

My live-in grandmother taught me the lessons of being a gentleman. She instructed me to open doors for women and to allow women to be seated before taking my seat, and to always walk closest to the street when walking with any woman. It didn't matter if the woman was friend or foe, friendly or antagonistic; I was taught to always be a gentleman. Grandmother taught me to treat all women as if they were my mother, sister, or daughter. I was instructed to "never, under any circumstances, hit a woman."

It was also Grandmother who taught me that "Peter Piper picked a peck of pickled peppers. If Peter Piper picked a peck of pickled peppers, where are the peck of pickled peppers Peter Piper picked?" She seemed pleased when I would correctly learn such limericks. Much to Grandmother's consternation, I would always end this little rhyme by saying kicked instead of picked.

"It's picked, not kicked. It's picked!" Grandmother would exclaim.

I would devilishly grin and promise to get it right the next time.

Grandmother and I would spend hours rehearsing my ability to memorize any assignment given to me. I didn't realize it then, but I would later come to know that I had a unique ability to memorize both written and spoken words.

My Mother

My Father

Mr. Charlie was an elderly man who lived around the corner. He was the neighborhood "old wise man." Mr. Charlie always wore faded blue jean overalls that appeared to be a few sizes too big. I don't remember ever seeing him without some type of hat on his—what must have been bald—head. Even at an early age, I loved to talk to the older occupants of my village.

"Good morning, Mr. Charlie. How are you doing this morning?"

A four year old child has very little to offer an older man, but he always stopped whatever he was doing to take the time to talk to me. Mr. Charlie taught me the value of expecting to accomplish great things.

He was the first person outside of my family to speak life into my future. I don't remember many of the specific things learned while sitting on Mr. Charlie's wooden back porch steps. And while I cannot recall the content of most of our conversations, I do remember always wanting to go back to talk with him.

Mr. Charlie always made me feel special. He seemed to know everything and I never tired of asking him questions. Sometimes I would just sit and watch him as he cleaned his string beans or tended to his garden. He would then sit in his rocking chair and freely dispense his unlimited wisdom. For instance, there was the time he told me that I would one day catch up with my older next door neighbor in school. I hadn't yet started kindergarten and David was already in the first grade. I don't know how Mr. Charlie knew, but David and I would eventually graduate from high school in the same year. Mr. Charlie was the first person outside of my home who I knew believed in me. He was the first man outside of my family to psychologically invest in my future.

My earliest recollections of school include graham crackers, Kool-Aid, and recess. Our favorite recess games were tackle football, tether ball, and basketball. Our kindergarten classroom was adorned with the alphabet being placed around the room on 8 X 11 inch sheets of paper. We learned how to put letters together to spell cat, dog, and hat. I remember hoping that my teacher would put my best work on the wall for PTA meetings.

My teacher had us read a book about a dog named Spot who was constantly running. I learned how to read somewhere amidst graham crackers, alphabet cards, and a running dog. I also had books at home that my mother encouraged me to read out loud. I read books to my mom and grandmother about Jack and Jill or Little Boy Blue. I came to enjoy reading out loud and always tried to put emotion and energy into those reading exercises. It seemed to make anyone who took the time to listen to me happy.

In school I often volunteered whenever the teacher needed someone to read. I later understood that my desire to read out loud was allowing me to develop an appreciation and an ability to speak publicly.

Every Saturday morning my father would take me to Mr. Hunt's barbershop. Mr. Hunt was an elderly man who had the best posture of anyone I had ever seen. His tall, slender body was always perfectly upright as he went about the business of making the neighborhood men presentable. The barbershop was actually converted from a garage, which was separated from Mr. Hunt's house. Because the side of his property bordered a residential street, access to the shop was easy.

There were three barber chairs in the shop and enough waiting chairs for seven patrons. Many times patrons would come to the door of the crowded shop, look in, and then promise to come back later. The smell of aqua velvet aftershave permeated the shop. Mr. Hunt always had the latest copies of *Sports Illustrated*, *Newsweek*, *Life*, *Jet* and *Ebony* magazines. Leafing through the magazines always made the wait seem a little shorter.

I absolutely loved to hear the men of the neighborhood talk to and about each other. I loved to sit in the corner chair and listen to these men argue with much enthusiasm about the war, politics, and sports. Mr. Hunt never let things get too personal, but there were occasional debates about the different philosophies of Martin Luther King and Malcolm X.

The men would play checkers, and God pity the poor loser of such matches.

"Now don't take this whuppin' personal."

"Shut up, old man. If you ever dream about beating me, you better wake up, call me, and apologize."

Good humored ridicule was the order of the day. I would often laugh to myself, but never too loud, less the ridicule suddenly turn to me. I didn't understand it then, but the barbershop taught me the value of healthy debate and being able to think fast when engaged in such debate.

Outside of my immediate neighborhood and home, my childhood experiences were diverse and generally positive. Through little league football, I discovered that I had a degree of athletic ability. I played for the infamous West Mound Rams. I played defensive and offensive end. My parents never came to my games, but I remember being extremely proud the time one of my father's coworkers told him about how I had scored a touchdown.

My father came home from work happy to discuss my achievements on the football field. "I heard that you scored a touchdown last week."

"Yes, sir. I did."

"Good job."

I didn't realize it then, but I constantly began to seek out opportunities to receive public approval. It made me feel good and I increasingly found ways to publicly perform. Maybe it was a substitute for the approval I wanted from my father. As a result, decades later I was sure to be a constant fan at all of my sons' athletic endeavors.

Through the church choir and the music program at school, I discovered a great love for music. Most of the boys in my neighborhood dreamed of playing in the NBA or NFL. I began to dream of singing with big bands like the ones who accompanied Nat King Cole or Frank Sinatra. Whenever my mother traveled back to her home church in Philadelphia, I accompanied her and she sometimes made sure that I sang a solo for the congregation.

"I believe for every drop of rain that falls, a flower grows. I believe that somewhere in the darkest night, a candle glows."

I was so proud the day I made all-city choir. It enabled me to sing with literally thousands of elementary, middle school, and high school students from all over the state at the annual music festival performed on the campus of The Ohio State University.

At church I began to sing solos and enjoyed the attention that I received. People in church really seemed to love and make a big fuss over little kids who could sing. I joined the school band and found that I had a unique ability to hear notes. I learned to play the clarinet and saxophone without really mastering the discipline of reading music. If I heard a song, I could figure out how to play it.

Growing up in the decades of the 60s and 70s, I was surrounded by the melodic sounds of great Motown artists like Diana Ross and the Supremes, Marvin Gaye, the Temptations, and Stevie Wonder. Gospel artists such as the Hawkins Family, James Cleveland, Mahalia Jackson, and Andre Crouch filled the radio airwaves. My favorite vocalist was the incomparable Donny Hathaway. In my heart,

I knew that I would one day be just like him, mesmerizing audiences with my smooth melodic melodies. I envisioned big stages with a full orchestra and adoring audiences.

The 60s and 70s also taught me that if you had the courage to lead, you must also have the courage to die. Medgar Evers, four students at Kent State, the Freedom Riders, Dr. Martin Luther King Jr., Malcom X, John F. Kennedy, Robert Kennedy, Schwerner, Goodman, Chaney, and countless other brave men and women whose names never made the news, paid the ultimate price for their desire and courage to lead.

Chapter Three

Singing, Studying, and Standing Out

In junior high school, I was selected to be in ensemble a year before I was officially eligible to be considered for such an honor. Our ensemble was a selection of the top sixteen singers in the school. My music teacher was a petite, chocolate, twenty-something year old woman named Mrs. Robinson. She was the most beautiful woman I had ever seen. Her big brown eyes were protected by extraordinarily long eyelashes that she seemed to use to get her students' attention. We came to understand that when her eyelashes were rapidly moving, she was not happy with what was happening.

She was often pleased with my contributions to the tenor part of whatever song we were singing. Pleasing this beautiful woman made music my favorite subject.

Academically, I had done well in elementary school. My grades and test scores warranted placement in one of two Hilltonia Junior High seventh grade honors homeroom classes. Mrs. Campbell, my seventh grade English teacher, was a small, frail woman with a head of very neat silver hair. She always walked as if she was in a hurry to get to wherever she was going. She seemed to be older and wiser than any other teacher in the school.

Mrs. Campbell wore wire rimmed glasses and always maintained constant eye contact whenever addressing a student. She expected total compliance with her expectations. Anything less would result in a public and severe rebuke.

Mrs. Campbell demanded her students give their best in her class. This elderly woman taught me the difference between giving my best and just doing enough to get by.

While there were times in middle school and high school where I did just enough to get by, I was aware of my slothfulness. I sometimes, however, simply didn't care.

My father's reactions to my grades were often one-sided. I would be severely punished for bad grades, but never rewarded when I brought home good grades. My father believed that his leather belt was the most effective way to motivate me to do my best in school.

While I never heard my mom and dad argue about anything, there sometimes seemed to be an underlying tension in our little house. I suppose it was partly the cause of my parents divorcing when I was twelve years old.

My father took me on a two-hour walk to tell me that he was leaving. I literally cried throughout that night until there were no more tears. I resolved the next morning that I would never cry again.

I missed my dad being in the house, and yet there was a welcomed calm in the household. I had come to enjoy watching boxing, football, and big time wrestling with my dad. There were, however, some benefits of him being gone. Certainly the leather belt would no longer be a part of my experience, as I don't recall ever being spanked again after the divorce.

I asked one of my Sunday school teachers, Elder Eugene Lundy, to be my Godfather. It never occurred to me that this was an inappropriate thing to do. Elder Lundy, however, was a med school student with a wife and four kids of his own. The fact that on his way to becoming a cardiologist he found the time to listen to the musings of my childhood, is a gift that I will never be able to repay. At an age where I needed a strong male figure for guidance, he stepped in and took the time to bless me with his wisdom.

Learning can be described as a relatively permanent change in behavior that occurs as a result of an experience. The learning experience does not happen in a vacuum. It cannot be confined to neighborhood and/or classroom experiences. Sometimes life lessons are learned because of the age in which one grows up.

The learning process is a part of life. Children growing up in the 60s and 70s experienced a violent political and social country. Racism was overt and often violent. On the evening news we witnessed summer riots, war protests, political and civil rights assassinations, hangings, and beatings. It was a time of social violence and turmoil.

In retrospect, I believe that I had a great childhood. Socially I had close friends that sometimes allowed me to travel between seemingly unrelated worlds. I felt totally comfortable with church friends and friends that would never set foot in a church. My friends consisted of good kids, "bad" kids, black kids, white kids, would-be athletes and musicians, a few kids destined for greatness, and a few kids destined for jail. These childhood experiences should have provided a strong self-image.

The inhabitants and experiences of my village were full of good will toward the children of the village. I never experienced feeling less than or somehow deficient because of my childhood experiences, and yet I was not strong enough to totally believe in my capacity to define my post high school potential. Oh how I wish that I had learned to see myself as the strong-willed person that I would eventually become before meeting with my high school counselor. While the inhabitants of my village believed in me and occasionally even celebrated my accomplishments, I soon came to know that my self-image was not as strong as it should have been.

Chapter Four

You're Not Good Enough

West High School, which opened in 1908, was one of the oldest and largest high schools in the city. The three-story brick building, along with its football field, took up an entire city block. The school was experiencing the impact of busing regulations designed to more equally disperse racial diversity throughout the city. West High had always had a small majority of minorities. Changing the demographics of the school did not occur without significant debate and occasional violence.

"Hey, nigger, where you think you goin'?"

I saw the barrel of what appeared to be a rifle crawl out of a car window. I then felt a burning sting in my leg. Fortunately, the weapon was just a BB gun. The car sped off. I learned that it was unwise to undertake the three mile walk home without the company of those who could at least act like they would fight if necessary.

By tenth grade my interests were condensed to music, church activities, and the civil rights movement. These three interests shaped my experience during my high school years.

I met a community activist and radio disc jockey that added another focus to my life. Les Brown was the most powerful black man in Columbus, Ohio. He didn't hold an elected office and he wasn't president of any organization. Les Brown was the most powerful black man in Columbus, Ohio because he absolutely controlled the radio waves at WVKO 1580 on our AM dial.

If there was a case of police brutality, which there often was, Les would get on the air and compel citizens to attend the city council meeting that week to voice their concerns. Based simply on his requests, thousands would flood downtown to let the city council know that the people would not be silenced.

Les had a theatre studio on the east side of the city in the heart of the hood. He used the studio to hold court and teach young would-be actors how to deliver moving monologues. My sister, Dawnetta, had had the privilege of meeting Les personally. I'd always wanted to meet him, so one day I went to the studio. When I walked in there weren't many people there.

"Hello, young man. And what is your name?"

Whenever Les spoke, he always seemed to be smiling. Even with his welcoming smile, I sometimes dreaded the simple question he'd asked. My name was so unique that I was always asked to repeat myself.

"My name is Reuel . . . Reuel Barksdale. I'm Dawnetta's brother."

"Young man, have you ever done any acting?" Les asked me.

"Yes, sir. I have done a few things at my church."

Les reached into a bunch of papers on a coffee table and handed them to me. "Learn this monologue and come back to me when you have it down."

The three page monologue was entitled *The Last Mile*. It was a story about a man sentenced to die for a crime that he hadn't committed. He ultimately found salvation while strapped to an electric chair. I devoured the pages of that monologue, memorizing every word. Two days later I was back at the studio ready to show off, and that is exactly what I did.

Les was duly impressed and began to mentor me on how to most effectively deliver the monologue. I had not just impressed Les, I had discovered that I had an ability to stand up and control an audience without singing. I could speak, and I was now in love with my newfound ability.

My high school years were a blur. I had never seriously contemplated what would happen after high school. That would prove to be a big mistake.

Going anywhere near the principal's office was something to be avoided. I had visited the string of administrative offices before, and had come to know that nothing good ever came from such a visit.

I had been summoned to the counselor's office for a "chat." As I walked up the granite steps to the second floor administrative offices, I began to anticipate the reason for my summons. My grades were good enough to insure my graduation. My attendance, while not stellar, certainly didn't warrant a special summons. Maybe I was going to get some kind of award for being the only tenth grader good enough to make senior choir, or the only eleventh grader to make ensemble.

In fact, the choir room had become my sanctuary. I could sing, and while in that room, I had the respect of my peers.

Maybe Mrs. Georgington, my twelfth grade speech teacher, had told the administrative team about my prowess in giving phenomenally moving speeches. I began to think that maybe it would be a good meeting after all.

Arriving at the administrative offices with sweaty palms, I slowly opened the wooden framed double glass doors, signed in with the school secretary, and waited for my name to be called. My eyes slowly took in my uncertain surroundings. The waiting area was relatively empty.

There was a sick tenth grader waiting to be picked up by her parents. Steve, a friend of mine and a frequent visitor to the second floor offices, was waiting to see if his most recent offense would get him suspended. Pictures of past principals decorated one wall. None of them seemed capable of forming a smile. I finally sat down, cracked jokes with Steve, and for a moment, forgot that I, too, was perhaps awaiting some type of judgment.

The counselor stepped out of his office and motioned for me to come back. I wished Steve good luck and made my way to the counselor's office. He closed the door and instructed me to have a seat. I had learned to be respectful of teachers, administrators, or pretty much any person in a position of authority. I came to the counselor's office prepared with a steady supply of "yes, sirs" and "no, sirs." I wasn't sure of the nature of the visit, but I would soon find out.

It seemed that upon verification of impending graduation, it was customary for seniors to have an exit interview. While one would think that a high school counselor would seek to counsel high school students, the purpose of the visit was probably administrative numbers crunching. The school administration wanted to know the future plans of its graduating seniors. How many would go to college? How many would seek immediate employment? Who would receive scholarships, and to which colleges would the students attend? My immediate concern, however, was trying to get out of that office as soon as possible.

The interview began with the counselor asking about my post graduate plans. The truth of the matter was that I hadn't given it much thought. I knew that when any adult asked what I intended to do after high school, the safe answer was always, "I want to go to college."

In reality, I didn't know what a credit hour was. No one in my immediate family had ever graduated from a four year institution. While I believed that I had above average intelligence—
after all, I had originally been placed in the accelerated home room—
my grades were average at best. There were things that were important to me, but my grades were not always on the "important things" list.

I convinced myself that my life would consist of becoming a very successful and wealthy singer. I'd always loved the world of music and I was known, at least around my community, for being able to really sing.

The counselor sensed that he had lost my attention and asked a follow-up question. "Have you given any thought to what you will do immediately after graduation?"

Without further hesitation I confidently declared, "I want to go to college."

I had not noticed the file on the counselor's desk. As he picked the slightly worn manila folder up, I noticed my name typed on the cover. It seemed as if he opened the file in slow motion. Without any trace of facial expression, he began to silently read for what seemed to be an eternity. Slowly he lifted his eyes from the file and confronted my bewildered stare. I will never forget the words that so easily flowed from this man's mouth.

"College? Young man, I don't think that is what you want to do. You don't want to go to college. What you need to do is to get a job."

I can't tell you what was said after those words. My mind must have gone numb. Somehow, in that moment, all of the lessons that my village had afforded me disappeared. I don't know why I couldn't hear Malcolm and Martin telling me to believe in myself. I don't know why my seventh grade placement into the honors class didn't come to mind. I somehow forgot the standing ovations for singing or remembering moving monologues. I couldn't hear Ms. Robinson's voice telling me how special I was.

This man who didn't really know me, and certainly didn't love me, was telling me what I did not have the capacity to do. He was telling me that I wasn't good enough to go to college. My village had given me so much love and affirmation, and yet somehow I was unprepared to fight this silly man.

I don't remember leaving the counselor's office. I don't remember talking to any of the inhabitants of my village about what this man had told me. I do remember that three months after graduation, I was working on line one in the Westinghouse Appliances factory.

West High School

Those Granite Steps to the Administrative Offices

Chapter Five

Making a Living

My shift began at 6:00 AM and ended a 2:00 PM. I'd never been a morning person, but where else could an eighteen year old make the kind of money I was making? My salary enabled me to drive a nice car and help Mom out with the bills. Having a significant amount of money every paycheck without a significant amount of bills was a wonderful way to live.

I was working beside men, and a few women, who had mortgages and adult responsibilities. I was still living at home with my mom, so they saw me as a kid. I didn't mind at all.

In retrospect, I see that the situation could have actually turned out to be a trap. How many young people never seek to develop their potential because of an early pursuit of paycheck over purpose?

In time I learned to hate Sunday nights because they were too closely connected to Monday mornings. Factory workers walked into the factory—faces expressionless—as if going off to war. The factory didn't seem to be a place to pursue passion or purpose. The factory was a place to pursue a paycheck.

The pay was good, but for newcomers who had not yet accumulated the seniority to warrant easier assignments, the work was physically demanding. Various appliances were made throughout the plant. Line one was where Westinghouse refrigerators were made.

The plant seemed to be the size of three football fields. The structure consisted of steel rafters, concrete walls, cement floors, and dirty windows. A steady hum of the banter of grown men who had long ago resigned themselves to a tedious life of mundane work filled the aging factory. The clanking of steel, an occasional horn signaling a pause in activity on the line, and the musty smell of old wooden pallets and electrical machinery completed the ambiance of my work world.

As refrigerators came down the assembly line, workers placed the shelving, trays, lights, and various compartments into the refrigerator. My job on line one consisted of, as refrigerators reached my station, continuously lifting refrigerators from their lying flat position to an upright position. The work was hard and unforgiving. If I got behind on lifting, the entire process of line one came to a halt.

The foreman was direct and uncompromising in his directives. If a worker couldn't get the job done, he would find someone who could. Many of my coworkers found a way to exist and flourish on the line. I wondered if I could survive in such an environment. Something in my spirit told me that I was destined to do more.

Chapter Six
College is Calling Me

One day while lifting refrigerators, the words of my high school counselor flooded my mind.

"You don't want to go to college. What you need to do is to get a job."

What if he was wrong? What if college was something that I could do? That question and the subsequent answer made all of the difference in my life.

That day after work, physically exhausted, I walked to the cafeteria, put my head on one of the tables, and fell asleep. Two hours later when I woke, my decision was clear.

I didn't yet know how to begin college. I still didn't know what a credit hour was or how many of them it would take to earn a degree. I did, however, know that I didn't want to lift refrigerators for the next forty years.

One day after work, I gathered the courage to apply to The Ohio State University. In the spring of 1974, less than a full year after my graduation from high school, I became a part-time college student. I worked during the day and found late afternoon classes to begin my academic journey. My days were long and demanding, but I was a college student and it felt good.

Two quarters after my enrollment into The Ohio State University, I was laid off at Westinghouse. The layoff allowed me to become a full-time student. Everything about the campus of The Ohio

State University was fascinating to me. The early twentieth century buildings seemed the perfect residence to house the wisdom of great writers, philosophers, and thinkers.

I loved the atmosphere of the student union where students met to eat, socialize, study, or to just hang out. I loved the excitement of the campus during the spring when the weather warmed and students came out in droves to throw Frisbees on the "yard" or ride their bicycles to class. I loved the electricity in the air when fall came and football season started. I loved my professors who seemed to be among the smartest people in the world.

Many of my professors had written multiple books. I'd never met an actual author before. I loved the debates that often occurred within the classroom. I actually loved going to the library, finding a quiet spot, and completing my homework assignments.

It didn't take long for me to realize that the magical, mysterious, and wonderfully mystical institution of higher education was a place where I belonged. I had never felt that type of energy fueled by the joy of learning things that made my world a place of growth and development. I felt perfectly at home in this wonderful world where my counselor had determined I didn't belong.

College was a place of discovery, and I was ready to discover. The words of my high school counselor soon faded from my consciousness. I discovered many things that had been unavailable for inspection in my limited experience, environment, and exposure. I met students from all over the world who had different experiences and ideas of what was and was not important in life.

I started to become involved in student activities, and in the fall of 1975, I was elected President of The OSU Gospel Choir. I read books to prepare for lectures that challenged the narrow paradigms of my small village. More importantly, I took tests, completed papers, and participated in classroom discussions that assured me I was indeed college material. College is where I discovered the absolute necessity of believing in my ability to achieve. I would never again allow anyone tell me what I couldn't or shouldn't do.

My favorite professors were Dr. Charles Nesbitt, Dr. William Nelson, and Dr. Frank Hale. These men were the smartest men that I had ever met. They were highly educated. They were articulate. They were accomplished, and they were black.

Dr. Nelson was a compelling oratory who often looked out the window while delivering his lectures. His words were so compelling that he always had the total attention of his students. Dr. Nelson was also known for his toupees, which never seemed to rest atop his head exactly right.

Dr. Hale had a vocabulary that rivaled Webster himself. One need not go to his class without a pocket dictionary in hand. At times it felt as if he must have read every book ever written.

Dr. Nesbitt was the youngest of my three role models. His lectures demanded that any student be prepared to answer questions pertaining to the subject of the day. An incorrect or unprepared answer was followed by momentary silence before the next student was given a chance to shine or go down in flames.

These men became my role models. These men believed in me and I worked hard to show them that their beliefs were well-founded.

On October 27th of 1975, with the help of my brother, who always had a connection or two, I became employed at Continental Insurance Companies. In retrospect, I now appreciate the reality that Ronnie was willing to help his little brother not only because he loved me, but because he also believed in my ability to not embarrass him. Because of the company's tuition reimbursement program, I now at least had a way to fund my education, so I gratefully continued college as a part-time student.

Chapter Seven

Thou Shalt Not . . .

Growing up in a very strict Pentecostal household, we were taught that while God was a God of love, doing anything that went against the teachings of the church was a sure ticket to hell. Because of these teachings, throughout my high school years I never smoked a cigarette, uttered a word of profanity, had a drink of alcohol, or committed adultery. We weren't allowed to dance, listen to secular music, play cards, or go to the movies.

As mentioned before, my father was an extreme disciplinarian. His words were never questioned, and it was a good idea to understand and obey his unspoken thoughts as well. While I am thankful for the self-discipline that I learned, my childhood of "thou shalt nots" caused me to make premature decisions.

My church taught that it was better to marry than to burn. I'm not sure which desire was stronger; my desire to make it to heaven, or my desire to avoid the torment of an everlasting hell.

"I'll never get married." I don't know why I told my friends that, but I was convinced it was true.

Many of the same adults who were warning against the sins of adultery were advising against the perils of getting married too young. Talk about an ethical dilemma!

In 1977, at the tender age of twenty-one, I decided to get married. My wife, whom I had met at church, was nineteen. We were in love and believed that our relationship was strong enough to endure whatever challenges life might decide to throw at us. I am certain there are marriages that are successful when young people around that age marry. My guess is that most young people would be better served by waiting until they have matured and are ready for such a major adult responsibility.

By the age of twenty-six, my wife and I were the proud parents of three beautiful boys. Our sons became the center of our lives. I decided early in their lives that I would never allow anyone to tell them what they could not do or what they would not become.

My job at Continental Insurance, coupled with the responsibilities of parenthood, affected my abilities to focus on my education.

The boy's mother and I enjoyed watching the boys grow and attending their football, basketball, soccer, and track activities. We determined that if our sons were involved in any activity, we would certainly be there. Not only was I committed to seeing their games, I made it a point to visit as many of their practices as possible.

Today, I am proud to say that they have grown up to be strong men. I think the aspect of their lives that most interests me is the fact that whether coaching football, basketball, or track, or teaching math at an alternative school, each of them have fallen in love with the beauty of teaching.

I have always had a strong work ethic. By the age of twelve I had a sizeable paper route, five regular lawn care customers, and a savings account that allowed me to buy my own bicycles and stylish clothes.

Shortly after I turned sixteen, I purchased my first car. It was an important purchase, as my single mother did not drive, and public transportation was our primary means of transportation. This work ethic was what later allowed me to be successful at Continental Insurance where I had a twenty year career. This work ethic allowed me to be successful in almost any work endeavor.

Chapter Eight
Am I Good Enough to Succeed?

When I first started working at Continental Insurance, I was a rate and code clerk. Continental was a three-story, beautiful brick building that, with its beautifully landscaped surroundings, occupied an entire city block. The two-story foyer consisted of a marble floor with a circular entrance that greeted its agents.

My job was to determine the premiums of our customers and then place those premiums into our computer system. My beginning salary was $105.00 a week. My take-home pay was actually less than my unemployment check from the factory. The training for the job consisted of listening to a "seasoned" employee talk in insurance jargon using a series of acronyms.

"Now line one is code fifty-one, which is the BI line the rate of which is not determined by the age of the vehicle, but by the characteristics of the insured."

She might as well have been speaking a foreign language.

I took a lot of notes and acted like I knew what this woman was talking about. My first supervisor was a middle-aged woman that had worked for the company for over ten years. She was a hands-on supervisor that was always watching everything.

"Where did you go?" "When will you be done?" "What are you working on now?" "Why is it taking you so long to finish that file?"

Anyone of these questions was fair for a supervisor to ask. The accumulation of these questions sometimes became burdensome. My supervisor began to question my abilities toward my clerical job. At one point I was put on probation and told that if my performance didn't improve, my job would be in jeopardy.

I continued to go to school at night and dream about one day working in one of the big offices on the top floor of the Continental building. I eventually transferred from The Ohio State University to Franklin University, a local business school that catered to adult students in search of a night program. There were times when I was so tired that after a day of work and school, upon finally reaching my home I would literally fall asleep in my driveway.

Accomplishing a task that takes longer than anticipated can be an agonizing process. There were many days when it seemed that progress was slow and problems were plentiful. I continued to work hard during the day and soon began to experience a series of firsts.

"Reuel, you have worked here for one year now. Where do you see yourself in five years?"

The Human Resources Manager was asking what seemed to be a casual question. I wasn't prepared with an answer, but instinctively knew that I should say something that indicated some thought on my part.

"I see myself becoming a Special Agent."

I really didn't know what a special agent was, but I knew that they drove company cars and had an expense account. Seeing that my car was barely making it to work, a company car would be a godsend. The job required that I go from a clerical position to a salaried professional position.

"Reuel, when you finish your third year of college and have completed two years of service with the company, we will count that as the equivalent of a bachelor's degree. This will allow you to apply for our career training program, which is a fast track to our professional positions."

I saw a way to succeed, and I was determined to pursue it. Eventually I became the first black Special Agent in the Columbus branch office. The responsibility required that I represent the company to independent agents selling our property and casualty products. I was given the largest territory in the branch. I didn't realize the significance of the assignment at the time, but these agencies run by wealthy white men had never dealt with an African American sales representative. I was, in fact, a first.

I'm not sure exactly when or how it happened, but my self-confidence was now secure. The self-doubt that had required me to question my abilities to even go to college was a distant thing of the past. I began to conduct seminars throughout the country to enable wealthy white men to sell our products. They listened to me and sometimes thanked me for my shared expertise.

I was subsequently promoted to the Midwest Regional Sales and Marketing Training Manager, becoming the first black person from the branch to report directly to home office. My responsibilities included providing sales and marketing training to a five state region. I soon began to travel across the country training both employees and agents on our sales and marketing strategies. I discovered that I had a real talent for that type of work.

For at least a year I was on the road sixty percent of the time. Airports, hotels, and rental cars became my new norm. I occasionally found a way to take my family with me.

One day while sitting in my third floor office, I received a visit from one of the home office Vice Presidents. Steve Zito was in town to meet with the regional brass. In my new position of Regional Sales and Marketing Manager, I had traveled the country delivering sales training for Steve. My meeting with this man literally changed the direction of my life.

Mr. Zito stated that he wanted to promote me to Assistant Vice President and move me to the home office in Piscataway, New Jersey. My mind immediately went into a whirlwind of thoughts. I had never lived outside of Columbus, Ohio. I didn't know anybody in New Jersey. I was involved in various church and community organizations in Columbus. My boys would have to leave their schools and their friends behind. My wife would be isolated from her friends and family.

These were all valid concerns, and yet a larger question remained.

What if I moved to home office and failed; what if I didn't have what it took to take on a position with national responsibilities?

Steve was going to be in town for a few days, which gave me some time to consider his offer. I don't think that I slept much over the next few days. When the time came to give my response, I had one question.

"What if I fail?" I asked Steve.

He calmly looked at me and said four simple words that will forever leave me indebted to him. "I won't let you."

There are times when all of your hard work seems to miraculously pay off. After eleven years with the company, in the summer of 1986 I was promoted to Assistant Vice President of the Continental Insurance Companies and moved my family to North Brunswick, New Jersey. It had taken eleven years of attending classes at night, changing majors, and progressively challenging positions at Continental Insurance, but in 1986 I was also awarded a Bachelor of Science Degree in Business Administration from Franklin University.

My national responsibilities were to provide sales and marketing training to our employees and independent sales agents. I traveled across the country conducting three-day sales seminars. I met with national vendors to determine what training tools were most effective. I met with regional vice presidents to create strategies to implement sales training within their specific regions. I also was given responsibility for our National Career Training Program, which selected college graduates to enter an intense 90-day training program and subsequently become underwriters or claims representatives.

I became accustomed to staying in high priced hotels in New York City and to being picked up from and driven to airports in limousines. While my corporate career was flourishing, my constant time on the road, coupled with the difficulties of getting married before either of us was really mature, began to take a toll on my marriage.

In the spring of 1989, I accepted the position of Regional Assistant Vice President of Human Resources for the Midwest Region. I was the head of Human Resources for a five state region. The new position allowed for me to move back to Columbus, Ohio. By the summer of 1992 I was divorced.

Chapter Nine

I'm Definitely Good Enough

As a young man, I had dreamed of becoming many things. I created visions of being a secret serviceman, a lawyer, a politician, a social activist, or an internationally known singer. I concocted visions of being someone who would somehow make a phenomenal impact on the world. Being a college professor had never been a part of my imagination, and yet little did I know it had always been my destination. In 1992, I obtained a Master of Science in Administration from Central Michigan University. In 1993, a miraculously strange thing happened. A coworker I had known for several years, and who was teaching at Franklin University, approached me.

"Hey, Reuel, have you ever thought about teaching? Franklin is looking for a Business Management adjunct professor for their evening program. If you are interested, I can get you an interview."

I had considered the possibility of teaching one day, but I always saw teaching at the college level as something that would happen in the distant future. Nonetheless, I interviewed for the positon, thereafter accepting an adjunct professor position at Franklin University. My reality had shifted from believing that I could not handle the academic rigors of college, to being an integral part of the higher education process. Attending The Ohio State University allowed me to discover that I belonged in college. Becoming an adjunct professor was an even greater revelatory experience. Not only did I belong in college, the world of academia needed me.

I soon realized that I was a gifted teacher. I was only teaching one night a week, but I soon came to understand that I was born to teach! My oratory skills, my love of debate, and my ability to engage an audience made me seek more teaching opportunities. In addition to my Franklin University assignment, I started teaching one night a week at a local community college. Columbus State Community College had younger students, many of whom were still trying to figure out their career pursuits.

At the age of thirty-eight, I was an Assistant Vice President of a fortune 500 company. My job afforded me a certain level of prestige, power and privilege, and yet I became totally engrossed in the process of teaching. I began to imagine teaching full-time after retirement. While retirement was at least twenty years away, teaching seemed like the perfect profession post corporate life.

Thoughts are a powerful thing. I have come to believe that our thoughts are not just random nonconsequential occurrences. They do, in fact, affect our lives.

Every job has duties and responsibilities that would be avoided if at all possible. My job was no exception to the rule. Whenever there were mass layoffs within the region or an office was closing, as the regional Human Resources officer, it was my job to deliver the news. In time I came to appreciate this uncomfortable responsibility.

I'll never forget one employee in particular. During her thirty year career with the company, her husband had died, her children had moved away, and her job was the only constant in her life. With tears in her eyes she had but one question: "Will the building still be here? They're not going to tear it down are they?"

"No, ma'am. To the best of my knowledge, the new company is going to maintain a presence in this building."

With that assurance, she faintly smiled, rose to her feet, and walked away.

At least I would be able to deliver the news while maintaining sincere empathy and affording the unfortunate recipients of the bad news some level of professional dignity.

When Continental Insurance was acquired by CNA Insurance, the layoffs were fast and furious. In October of 1995, I, myself, was laid off. I had worked for the company for twenty years and now I was faced with the daunting task of figuring out what was next. In a span of three years I lost my job, my marriage, and my home.

Chapter Ten
Living My Making

How difficult could it be for someone like me to get another job at an executive level? After all, I had twenty years of corporate experience and a master's degree. I began to use the skills that I had extolled to the hundreds of people that I had counseled at my now former employer. I sharpened my resume, inventoried my contacts, and looked at finding a new job as a full-time job.

Meanwhile, I started a consulting business with the hopes of maybe creating a lucrative consulting firm. I'd never liked rollercoasters. The consulting world, however, is a big rollercoaster consisting of really lucrative months, followed by months of financial drought.

I was teaching part-time at Franklin University and Columbus State Community College (CSCC). I was earnestly trying to find a corporate position similar to the one that I had just left. Fortunately that never materialized.

In January of 1997, I accepted a full-time position as an Instructor at CSCC. In 1998 I married for the second time. In 2000 we built a house. My life was coming back together. It seemed that everything that I had lost was being restored.

I wanted to perfect my ability to teach. I wanted to fully understand the world of higher education. I enrolled in the Higher Education Administration PhD program at The Ohio University.

Throughout my life God has blessed me with men that have spoken life to me. Even though I had successfully matriculated through a bachelor's degree and master's degree program, I wondered if this kid from the little house on the west side of Columbus could actually be accepted into a doctorate program at a major college.

My pastor, Bishop Timothy Clark, is one of the most phenomenal preacher/teachers in the world. I approached him with my concern.

"Pastor, I want to get into a PhD program at The Ohio University, but I don't know if I'll be accepted."

He said three words that calmed me and let me know that I was good enough. He looked at me and declared, "They'll accept you."

Three years later, I successfully completed my comprehensive exams. I carried a 3.62 GPA in my doctorate program.

Currently, I am a fully tenured professor in the Business Programs Department at CSCC. I have served as a faculty member at CSCC for nineteen years. In the spring of 2011, I was honored by Dr. David Harrison, President of Columbus State Community College, to be the only faculty member to ever provide the graduation commencement address. It can be viewed on YouTube at https://youtu.be/BYi01uBidYw.

In 2012, I received the Columbus State Community College Distinguished Teacher of the Year Award. In December of 2012, I was listed in *Ohio Magazine* as being an outstanding teacher and was identified as "An Excellence in Education Honoree." In addition to my teaching responsibilities at CSCC, I coordinate the Human Resources Management Degree program and served on various committees. Columbus State Community College currently has a major initiative to work with local high schools to improve the graduation rates and college attendance rates of Central Ohio high schools students.

One of the committees formed to address this initiative was the West High School Learning Community, of which I became a member in the spring of 2015. Learning Communities were being designed to assist students in attaining stronger academic skills as well as forming support networks while adjusting to their first semester at CSCC. This initiative is critical to increasing the enrollment and success of inner-city public school students. Many of these students find themselves in a situation similar to my high school experience; a situation that does not include parents with higher education experience.

On July 27, 2015, I, along with five other representatives from CSCC, traveled to West High School to meet with various faculty members and administrators of the high school. It was the first time that I had been in the school in over forty years. Most of my fellow Learning Committee members from CSCC had never been inside of the school. The meeting was held in a lab used to teach electronics. That particular class did not exist when I was a student at West.

During the meeting, we sat around a very long table and talked about the current challenges of the students at West High. I learned that approximately thirty-five percent of the students failed to graduate.

After our meeting we were given a tour of the building. When we arrived at the student advisors' offices, my mind revisited the conversation of over forty years ago. I smiled having the knowledge that my high school counselor was wrong. He was wrong!

I sometimes wish that I could have a conversation with him. I don't have a desire to gloat or to prove him wrong, but to suggest that more care should have been taken in potentially destroying the education and career paths of those under his influence. In the eyes of my high school counselor, I had not been overly successful in school. My past experiences led him to the incorrect conclusion that my academic pursuits should come to an abrupt end. He felt comfortable in judging my future life possibilities based on the contents of a manila folder with my name on it. I was, in his mind, destined to a life of skilled labor without the hope of experiencing education past my high school experience.

I exhale when I say that I no longer feel the need to simply make a living. I have been blessed for the last twenty years to live my making.

Teaching at Columbus State Community College

Conclusion

The Problem

Learning occurs as we experience life, reflect on what we have experienced, and subsequently make adjustments in our lives as a result of such reflection. We learn the value of money and it changes the way we manage our finances. We learn the value of time and we are empowered to be better managers of time. It could be argued that it is impossible to not learn. Life is full of lessons that force at least a minimal amount of learning to occur. The baby eventually learns to walk after multiple falls and failures to properly balance. While our parents hold our hands and coach us to move toward them, it is the child's gradual acquisition of balancing acumen that allows this fundamental motor skill to be learned.

We learn to speak a language by listening to those in our environment communicate, and reward us with smiles and laughter when we accurately make appropriate sounds. Chinese babies learn mandarin, Iranian babies learn Farci, Ugandan babies learn Swahili, and American babies learn English. None of these children chose which language they would speak. Their environment and their interaction with those in their environment help the child to learn the language that will enable them to properly communicate.

Parents are our first and perhaps most important teachers. Can you remember your parents pointing to your nose, eyes, and ears while imploring you to correctly identify each facial member? My parents taught me how to make my bed, tie my shoes, and to take out the trash on Tuesday mornings. My father taught me how to ride a bike without training wheels, and to never run away from a fight. My mother taught me to never speak to anyone out of anger, and to always show kindness to those who were less fortunate than me. My parents taught me the importance of attending church on a regular basis, doing tasks to the best of my ability, and the necessity of hard work.

At some point in our early childhood we learn to present images that are *acceptable* to those in our environment. It is at that point the child learns the value of the mask. A mask is a representation of a false but often preferable reality. "Don't embarrass me when we go into this restaurant. *Act* like you have some home training."

And so, it begins. The child temporarily puts on a mask and takes it off when dinner is over. The child goes to school and gradually learns to fit in by assimilating, adjusting, and acknowledging that the original self is not always accepted.

We have a headache or some type of intolerable pain, and yet when we are asked, "How are you doing?" the answer is almost always, "Fine." We once upon a time may have said, "I hurt" or "I'm going through something," only to find that transparency brought about a judgement or a contempt that simply wasn't worth the trouble.

We become accustomed to hiding our true self. No matter what we may be going through, we put on a mask that says, "I'm Okay." We gradually come to understand that, depending on the situation, there are various masks that may be worn to hide our vulnerabilities. We have a mask for our family, another mask for our friends, yet another mask for mere acquaintances. Then there is a more polished and shined mask when interacting in spiritual circles. We soon become so comfortable with our various masks that we put them on without even being conscious that we are wearing them. We weren't born wearing masks. This is something that we learn to do.

There are those that suffer from what I call mask identity. This occurs when one has worn a mask for so long that the mask becomes their self-image, and the original self is no longer recognized. Dreams are no longer recognized.

The Promise

Can you remember the dreams you had as a child? Can you remember the dreams you had of becoming something? What ever happened to those dreams? Can you go back and find them, or have they been forever lost in a sea of masks?

There is something tremendously liberating about individual growth. I am not referring to the type of growth accompanied by the attainment of college degrees or prestigious titles. Nor am I referring to the type of growth that comes from learning the tenets of a particular religion or from visiting the holy places of the patriarchs. I do not wish to negate the powerful benefits of these and similar experiences. I have devoted the majority of my life to regularly attending the church of my choice, being involved in church ministries, and following the religious teachings handed down to me by my parents.

Formal education, organized religion, and personal study are all great learning tools. I believe, however, that there may be additional experiences that lead to both intellectual and spiritual enlightenment. My personal journey has revealed this to be true.

I have passed a few tests and flunked a few others. Sometimes I wish that the lessons learned on my journey would have been learned at an earlier age. It seems as though my learning curve has been longer than necessary. Perhaps I didn't learn all of the lessons that were presented to me. And so the question of the moment is: What lessons are to be learned from the stories in this book? What have these maskless characters allowed the reader to more clearly see?

A closer look at each of the stories reveals that there was a process that led to a promise. The consistency found within these stories is that no matter what personal hell these individuals experienced, no matter what masks they wore, no matter what dreams they had and subsequently forgot, there was always—at the end of a process—a promise waiting to be fulfilled.

Through the prophet Jeremiah, God declares to his discouraged, despondent, and defeated people, *"For I know the plans I have for you, declares the LORD, plans to prosper you and not to harm you, plans to give you hope and a future"* Jeremiah 29:11 (NIV). **THIS IS THE PROMISE!**

Go back and get your forgotten dreams! Remember the forgotten hopes that have been crushed by the difficulties of your process and hidden by the masks that made you forget who you were born to be. Your problem is never as great as your promise!

You were born with the promise of a purpose, and that purpose cannot be erased by the pain of the process. Unlearn what you have learned so that you may know what you have always known. Your purpose is the promise that God has for you; a promise to give you a hope and a future. This, my friend, is the lesson beneath the mask.

About the Author

Reuel Barksdale is an established organizational development specialist with over twenty years of corporate experience. As an Assistant Vice President of a Fortune 500 corporation, he had direct responsibility for the design, development, implementation, and evaluation of organizational development strategies and activities. Mr. Barksdale was responsible for functional and operational responsibilities at regional and corporate levels for managing Human Resources, organizational development, and training in areas of sales and marketing, management and diversity.

Mr. Barksdale is currently a tenured full professor in the Business Programs Department at Columbus State Community College where he teaches Organizational Behavior, Human Resources Management, Business Management and Interpersonal Skills Management. He is also Coordinator of the Human Resources Development Degree and Certificate Programs. Mr. Barksdale has served as an adjunct professor at Ohio Dominican University and Franklin University and has been a guest lecturer at Otterbein College and The Ohio State University Todd A. Bell National Resources Center on the African American Male.

As a motivational speaker and organizational development consultant, Mr. Barksdale has addressed audiences across the country on the topics of change management, diversity management, strategic planning, leadership, and employee development.

Reuel Barksdale received his Bachelor of Science degree from Franklin University, and a Master of Science in Administration degree from Central Michigan University. With the exception of his dissertation, Mr. Barksdale finished the coursework necessary for his Doctorate in Higher Education Administration from Ohio University.

For booking information, please contact The Gold Standard Initiative at: tgsinitiative@gmail.com